The Daily Practice of Life

The Daily Practice of Life

PRACTICAL REFLECTIONS TOWARD
MEANINGFUL LIVING

Walt Shelton

CrossLink Publishing

CrossLink Publishing
1601 Mt. Rushmore Rd, STE 3288
Rapid City, SD 57702

Ordering Information:
Quantity sales. Special discounts are available on quantity purchases by corporations, associations, and others. For details, contact the "Special Sales Department" at the address above.

The Daily Practice of Life/Shelton —1st ed.

ISBN 978-1-63357-305-5

Library of Congress Control Number: 2020932400

Library of Congress Cataloging-in-Publishing Data Bible Study 2. Christian Commitment 3. Bible—Examination

First edition: 10 9 8 7 6 5 4 3 2 1

Praise for *The Daily Practice of Life*

Walt Shelton writes with a humanity that is refreshing in a world that can often leave folks feeling disconnected. He brings Christianity to his words in a way that feels inclusive of people of all faiths, yet he's very secure in his own religious tradition. He's a great storyteller, often bringing tales of his upbringing, wise dogs he's loved or even wiser family members who continue to teach him what it means to be a person of faith and an honorable human being. He always delivers a nugget, a reminder of the people we want to be. He's a joy to read.

Nicole Villalpando
Specialty Editor and Faith Editor
Austin American-Statesman

In this gentle and deeply humane collection of essays, Walt Shelton draws upon his own life experiences—as son, grandson, brother, husband, dad and granddad, as well as student, lawyer, teacher, pen-pal, dog lover, and dedicated runner and golfer—to meditate upon the challenges and joys of daily life. He uses texts as varied as the Synoptic Gospels, the writings of rabbis and monks, and songs by the Beatles, the Byrds, and the Traveling Wilburys to go beyond the currently fashionable emphasis on living "mindfully," which too often becomes but another form of self-absorption. Instead, Walt urges us simply to be responsibly "present" and connected to all that surrounds us—to nature, to those in our care and trust, and to all others who are in need. This thoughtful and thought-provoking collection is intended for believers and non-believers alike and could not be timelier.

Dr. Howard Miller
University Distinguished Teaching Professor Emeritus
Departments of History and Religious Studies
University of Texas at Austin

When you see the face of Walt Shelton, hear his voice, or read the pages of his book, *The Daily Practice of Life*, you will know that you have met a man committed to making a difference in the lives of others. Regardless of your faith tradition, you will find a common experience in the personal stories he shares. Woven in are references to scripture and other inspirational writings that encourage further reflection. In pondering the joys and challenges of living attentively and intentionally, Walt reminds us to be accepting, open and kind to family, friends, strangers, and even ourselves.

Johnnie Overton and Susan Holman
Church Women United
Austin, Texas

How does the path of an itinerant rabbi from the first century intersect with our lives? In this collection of intimate reflections on his own life, Walt Shelton shows us the way, with simplicity, grace and authenticity. Each chapter moves us beyond meditation into living life faithfully, loving all of our neighbors. Walt reminds us that tending to the teachings of Jesus expands our gaze outward to see God at work everywhere in people working for the common good.

Rev. Dr. John Elford
Senior Pastor
University UMC
Austin, Texas

Walt Shelton's writings and teaching have inspired me for many years. He draws from a variety of faith traditions discovering the commonalities we share. Walt brings out the spiritual and meaningful in everyday events. He truly lives the life of a disciple and freely shares Christ through his living. Each chapter of this book opens our eyes to see how we too can be a true follower of Christ.

Rev. Cheryl Hill-Kimble
Pastor of Highland Park Baptist Church
Affiliated with the Alliance of Baptists and Cooperative Baptist Fellowship
Austin, Texas

Walt Shelton delivers in this work cogent reflections on the matters of our lives that are informed by faith and ethical mores. I have watched Walt as a faculty colleague for over three decades. His gifts for teaching, his powers of discernment, and his exemplary life-modeling have blessed our students and our community. As a reader of this book, you are in for a treat.

Brad Toben
Dean of Baylor Law School

As Walt Shelton's law student, work colleague and friend, I have been blessed with over two decades of his influence on my life. He has now blessed us all with *The Daily Practice of Life*—a profound guide to a life of inclusion and authentic faith. So timely in an era of distorted politics and religion, this book embodies an amazing man and has a permanent place on my annual reading list.

Bane Phillippi
SVP and General Counsel, McCoy Corporation
Lieutenant Commander, U.S. Navy Reserve
Baylor Law School class of 1998
Former law student of Walt Shelton

I had the pleasure of having Professor Walt Shelton at Baylor Law School in several classes and the opportunity to work with him as a research assistant for a presentation to a statewide legal convention and a law review article. His depth of knowledge in his course subjects is impressive in its own right, but his skill in sharing knowledge is unmatched. Professor Shelton's thoughtful and enthusiastic approach makes one proud to be his student, which is like reading one of his columns and this book: engaging, thought-provoking, conversational, and—despite the complexity of the subject matter—comprehensible. Outside of the classroom, his kindness and compassion make the biggest impression. I regard Professor Shelton as an esteemed legal colleague, mentor, and friend. With his Statesman columns and publication of this book, readers will know what I and his other students have known for years—his wisdom and teaching extend far beyond the law and the classroom door.

Morgan Beam
Attorney
Tomball, Texas
Baylor Law School class of 2016
Former law student and research assistant of Walt Shelton

Nothing is more thoughtful and comforting, yet a call to action than Walt Shelton's writings. Who should care how many times you go to church, memorize the words of the service, and condemn all others who do not think like you or do not believe in "your God"? It is all very simple. Do you have an intentional, habitual implementation of your faith here on earth? Do you treat others with kindness and respect with active caring? Let Walt help you learn to make your faith authentic and be a true follower of Jesus in the here and now.

Ronald L. Beal
Professor of Law
Baylor Law School

When I read Walt Shelton's articles in the *Austin American-Statesman*, I feel like I just sat down with a good friend and heard advice from someone who truly cares about my well-being. Walt's thoughtful and applicable approach emphasizes how perspective and simple, purposeful acts of kindness profoundly impact our lives, including during times of joy and sorrow, as well as affecting others around us. Walt's slice of life stories share his path and invite his readers to find, modify, and improve their own.

Colette Barron Bradsby
Assistant General Counsel
Texas Parks and Wildlife Department, Austin, Texas
Baylor Law School class of 1992
Former law student of Walt Shelton (in the first course he taught at Baylor in 1990)

Paul urges us in Colossians to honor God through all aspects of our work. I have met few people who embrace their calling as much as Professor Shelton. His words in *The Daily Practice of Life* reveal an intimate portrait of a humble servant. But more importantly, they convey perspectives that are as enlightening as they are deeply relatable. *The Daily Practice of Life* reads as familiar as a conversation with a dear friend, and it shows us that a life well-lived is a creed that transcends the mission of Christian faith.

Jason Hill
Attorney
Baylor Law School class of 2004
Former law student of Walt Shelton

During law school, I had the privilege of taking several of Professor Shelton's classes. I walked away from those courses with a better understanding of the law, but the greatest lesson Professor Shelton imparted through his teaching and mentorship was mindfulness, a process that I've continued to use to help bring balance and focus to my life as a wife, mother, attorney, and naval officer. For those looking for a thoughtful and genuine approach to living an intentional life, I cannot recommend *The Daily Practice of Life* enough.

LCDR Alexandra Gioiello
JAGC
United States Navy
Baylor Law School class of 2018
Former law student and research assistant of Walt Shelton

Walt's teaching, like his columns, is rooted in his deep Christian faith, but he also explores how other religions have dealt with the common issues all persons experience in life. He asks readers to think in fresh ways about complex issues related to morality and religion.

Fred and Barbara Worley
Members of Walt's Journey class for more than fifteen years and of the prior interfaith Practical Faith group

This book is an excellent resource for thoughtful meditation and reflection. As an environmental attorney, Professor at Baylor Law School, and Bible scholar, Walt's insightful articles (now chapters of this book) give us reason to ponder our life journey and the difference we can make. He is both an excellent teacher and a committed Christian practitioner in everyday life. We are privileged to participate, now for more than twenty years, in the Journey class Walt leads. This book reflects many of his basic themes over the years in our group. While always rooted in the Bible, Walt also draws from a wide range of sources, including writers from Christian and other authentic faith traditions.

John and Suzanne Lowe
Members of Walt's Journey class for more than twenty years and of the prior interfaith Practical Faith group

To my wife, Roxanne, and our children, Rusty and Courtney: my role models

Very early in the morning, while it was still very dark, he got up and walked a long way out to a deserted place for a daily time of prayerful solitude. His close friends hunted for him but knew where to find him. They said that people were looking for him. He said: "It's time for us to go to work."

Gospel of Mark
(author's paraphrase of 1:35–38)

Contents

Acknowledgments

While space limitations prevent me from thanking everyone who helped me with my book, I express a heartfelt thank you to:

Rick Bates and all at CrossLink for believing in me as an author and for all their gracious, excellent work and assistance in the editing and publication process.

Mindy Reed for her expert developmental and traditional editing of my completed draft manuscript and for her support before I submitted it for potential publication.

Nicole Villalpando at the *Austin American-Statesman* for her longtime support, editing, and consistent encouragement to keep on writing.

The many *Statesman* column readers over the years who complimented my writing, expressed appreciation for offering input on faith-related issues, and encouraged me to compile them and write this book.

All of my Baylor Law students over the years. They challenged me with their intellect and questions, empowered me with their interest in the subject matter, pushed me to stay a step ahead of them, provided helpful input, and made me work to communicate effectively across generations, while utilizing my traditional approach toward teaching. Hopefully they made me a better teacher, which in turn made me a better and more careful writer.

All current and former members of the Journey class who share a faith and life journey each week together, digging deeply into important issues, listening respectfully to one another, and learning from differences of opinion.

My brother Rusty for his comments on many pre-*Statesman* column publications with an unparalleled grammatical and substantive command combined with his life of authentic faith.

My son Rusty and all of the crew at Zilker Media for their expert guidance for a new book author unfamiliar with the intricacies of publication possibilities and dynamics and for their ideas and work in promoting my book.

My daughter Courtney who complimented every one of my columns and strongly encouraged me to broaden my perspective to consider concepts from other faith traditions while holding fast to my own.

My wife Roxanne who read a prepublication draft of every column and enhanced its practicality, quality, and understanding.

On a more personal level, with thankfulness for their profound impacts on my writing and never-ending love and admiration to:

My parents, Jerry and Catherine Shelton, who crossed the bridge to the brighter light of the next life way too early. From an early age, they instilled by example an inclusive, respectful, and inquiring reverence for the Bible and living out our Christian faith.

My slightly older brother Rusty who has been my companion, advisor, friend, and example my entire life, including with his and his wife Julia's vibrant and relationship-changing couples' ministry, first in Atlanta and now in the Dallas area.

Our grandchildren from oldest to youngest—Luke, Brady, Bell, Chuck, and Sadie—for augmenting the quality of this wonderful grandparent life season and, when needed, restoring my perspective.

Our son-in-law Chad and daughter-in-law Paige for loving and caring for our children, being great parents to our grandchildren, and embracing me, my wife Roxanne, and all of our family.

Our children, Rusty and Courtney, for their love, support, encouragement, and special friendship now as adults, as well as demonstrating how to live qualitatively and with joy.

Roxanne—my wife, best friend, and life companion—for standing beside me always, unconditionally loving and caring for me, and showing me and anyone who crosses her path authentic faith in action every day.

Foreword

What does it mean to live a meaningful and fulfilling life as a Christian? Certainly worship and rituals play key roles, but the reality is that faith, character, and meaning are built and nurtured in daily living and action, endeavoring to follow the life and teachings of Jesus in practical action now that is rooted in love and care for others and informed by our life experiences.

We did not know it at the time, but our life experience with this kind of intentional living started early thanks to the model provided by our dad, Walt Shelton. He begins his daily routine far before the sun comes up. We remember his early mornings sipping coffee with our dog and reading, growing his faith and preparing for his many teaching obligations with diligence and care. His routine always includes exercise, time with us (especially important when we were children) and, importantly, he never misses an opportunity to get together with someone he cares about, from fellow church members to old friends or students he continues to mentor.

He also modeled intentional decisions about work, choosing a demanding and socially relevant career path with Environmental Law but working toward a balance that allowed him to be home for dinner at night. He lives mindfully, attending to others, caring for the environment, and holding awareness of people in his life who he cares for and has lost. Dad continues to remind us that actions speak louder than words and that faith grows as we live out the example of Jesus, rather than simply reading and talking about it. He also reminds us that what we say matters, because we can never fully take it back. His legacy is a lot to live up to and something we keep striving to attain. He serves as a model for humility, generosity, and working toward greater social justice.

This introduction would be insufficient without mentioning our mom, who also continues to teach us a tremendous amount about living well through service and awareness. Mom never met a stranger. Throughout our lives, she has consistently gone out of her way to serve people who are often ignored by others. Our parents form quite a team that has always been a model of Jesus's teachings about caring for our neighbors.

As adults now, we continue to work to implement lessons we learn from both of our parents, especially the importance of family, faith, and putting our beliefs and principles into daily practice. We may not get up as early as our dad, but we both incorporate many of his routines that help us live well, including service, exercise, and love of people and animals. With busy families and careers of our own, our dad's example has been invaluable in showing us how to carve out a life that fits with the values that are most important to us. Rather than feeling like the years are flying by without us being present, we have the gift of being mindful of all the ways we are blessed in life and how those blessings serve as a calling to put our feet to the pavement and help those around us.

Dad started writing faith and life related newspaper articles for the *Austin American-Statesman* in May of 2009 and has had them regularly published since then. They touch people from a variety of faith backgrounds and belief systems, inspiring them to consider important issues and, more importantly, live better, both for themselves and the good of others. Dad is our example of how to create a more meaningful life through intention and routine, and, for readers, this book will serve as an inspiration for how to create your own routines based on what matters most to you.

The chapters are brief to allow you to enjoy the book as an early-morning devotional or the basis of a faith/life related discussion group of any size. It also includes two appendices offering input and practical ideas related to the importance of intra-faith and interfaith small discussion groups. Dad draws from his experience leading such groups, including his over four decades leading his own Sunday School classes and other small discussion groups, including a vibrant interfaith group called "Practical Faith" that met in coffee shops for three years.

In a nutshell, *The Daily Practice of Life* is a book for those who want to take and implement a more intentional and open-minded approach to their faith and life journey. We are excited you have chosen to pick it up – we hope Dad's message is as meaningful to you as it has been to us.

— Courtney Morton and Rusty Shelton
2020

Preface

I think Jesus is a great example for anyone and everyone. By "Jesus," I mean the man in history who we can discover to a great extent through thoughtful reading of the Gospels, especially the earliest ones: Mark, Matthew, and Luke. As a Christian, Jesus is more than that to me. The more, however, does not overwhelm his model as a human being both in how he lived and what he taught. Sometimes for Christians, the stellar model for living now that Jesus provides can get lost in his deification and worship. I think the opposite should be true. My belief system about Jesus, which elevates him to the Lord I seek and worship, makes me pay closer attention to what he taught and how he showed us to live as a rabbi (and more so simply a person) in time. "Following" Jesus is about practical action now, rooted in love and care for others. Thus, within my faith tradition and understanding the sound-bite mentality of our current generation, I prefer the term "disciple" or "follower" to "believer" for a person who is Christian.

For people of any or no faith, Jesus is a wonderful source for a potentially authentic and meaningful life. This book includes an initial chapter centered on the daily practice of qualitative living, especially but not exclusively from a faith-based perspective. A collection of shorter and more focused chapters follows that offer some practical suggestions for thought and application. Many of them are based on certain aspects of the life and teachings of Jesus. Most of these writings were initially published on the weekly faith page of the *Austin American-Statesman* for about a decade between 2009 and 2019. They appear here primarily in the order of publication and with some minor changes to the texts since original publication. These chapters are partially autobiographic, drawing on experience and seeking to apply lessons learned to our common experience. What good is faith without practical application and day-to-day translation in our lives?

Our life experiences are important ingredients to our ongoing, changing, and hopefully, progressing faith journeys. Intentional, habitual implementation is what makes faith, or any belief system, truly authentic. Life is at its core a discipline. If we do not intentionally practice it each day, then we miss out on a more meaningful existence here on earth.

Recurrent themes and some favorite passages (and pet peeves) are conveyed throughout the book. Similarly, there are multiple references to certain learning and spiritually formative experiences in my life, such as my parents' divorce, my correspondence and friendship with a few prisoners, my love of dogs, and certain influential people, including other authors. Repetition of some biblical texts and references is intentional and without any effort to graft in other citations for variety. Cherry-picking and echoing especially meaningful words and teachings, such as the Sermon on the Mount, as well as the importance of social justice, are vital for keeping what is most important accessible each day.

While the minimal word count from each of the *Statesman's* short articles was a challenge, it helped me simplify my thoughts into short in-a-nutshell-like pieces. My hope is that readers benefit from this approach. Brevity allows readers to read, think about, and potentially respond to the thoughts in each segment. I also hope this gives way to discussions of intra-faith, interfaith, and qualitative life considerations and issues.

I have included two appendices at the end. They are intended to offer some insights and suggestions for small group study and dialogue based on decades of experience leading small discussion groups. My experience for the most part, but not exclusively, has been in small group settings in churches. The venue, however, for significant, diverse, and respectful dialogue is not so important. Rather, the habit of considering important issues in small chunks of time for real application in life is something that can contribute to making a difference and building important friendships.

Life, especially but not exclusively in a faith context, is indeed a practice. Intentionally sharing our one-time journey in quality time with others can make our path a more informed and especially rich time.

Walt Shelton

2020

CHAPTER 1

The Daily Practice of Life

Awakened again from the peaceful escape of deep sleep, I hammered the alarm off and stumbled out of bed into the shower. I toweled off while my canine buddy fulfilled his early morning ritual of licking my feet and lower legs dry. Finally, I opened my eyes. With the lights still off, I hurriedly dressed, certain that both socks were a dark match. Then, I grabbed some coffee and breakfast for the car, left the house, and sped out for another workday. Around mid- to late-morning, I felt somewhat awake but not fully attuned.

How we habitually spend our first waking hour of each day has a profound impact on how qualitatively—or not—we live. Being intentional about each day's new beginning is an important first step. Stumbling around in a rushed stupor usually insured for me a distracted, dysfunctional daily experience. I leaped from one project to the next, typically with my mind racing ahead to what was next and always preoccupied with just making it to the end of the day.

We set an attitudinal tone for each day in our early mornings or first-part-of-the-day time, whether it is 5:00 a.m. or 9:00 a.m. Will our experience in time be hectic or relaxed? Will we be focused and mindful or disordered and constantly looking ahead? At some point decades ago, I desperately needed and longed for a change in routine. What I needed was an *actual* routine in place of my early morning void.

Finding a model for daily preparedness, then experimenting with different schedules can progress toward a personal discipline that blooms into more meaningful day-to-day living. As a Christian, I look primarily to the life and teachings of Jesus as a guide. What I discovered years ago helped me with a morning process to increase my potential to be more fully present and engaged and to realize more opportunities. It also turned my first waking hour or two into my favorite part of the day.

Jesus gives us a great model for starting our day. Although the Gospels do not tell us a lot about his life, the first chapter of Mark gives us insight into how Jesus started his day. "In the morning while it was still very dark, he got up and went out to a deserted place, and there he prayed" (Mk 1:35). I imagine this verse is a summation of what Jesus did to start his day as a matter of developed habit. In the few verses that follow, the author of Mark informs us that Jesus's friends had to hunt him down. When they found him, he told them it was time to go to work. Thus, I believe that in part, Jesus's early morning process enabled him to live a life of daily service to others. In crowds and challenging circumstances, per accounts in the Gospels, Jesus managed to focus on one person in need at a time. That is how Jesus encouraged his followers to live per his actions and teachings. Indeed, actively loving and caring for others is the highest of vocations. It is our common calling in every legitimate faith tradition.

I asked myself some time ago: What does this predawn story in Mark practically offer me as instruction for living more completely? After trial runs and reflection, I discovered building blocks I could try to follow. First, Jesus was up "while it was still very dark," so I needed to start my day very early and become a so-called "morning person." Second, Jesus went so far out that his friends had to "hunt" for him. (And he did not have a car!) Therefore, I needed to exercise. I chose morning runs as my preferred form of movement. Third, he spent time in a "deserted place," so I needed solitude in a special place or places to be developed over time. Finally, "he prayed," so it was essential for me to be prayerful with thanksgiving and petitions, not only for my own day, but more especially for others in need. As a footnote, Jesus met with key friends at the close of his routine. Thus, if I could add a good friend or two for the start of my day, it might augment my experience and preparation for the rest of the day.

I continue to work on how to best translate the early morning foundation for the more effective life that I found in Mk 1:35. Currently, I start with coffee on a quiet porch with my faithful dog, who always models being and living in the present. I then move with a second cup of coffee in hand and dog in tow to my favorite chair in our small study, otherwise known as "my room." Usually, I read a chapter or two of the Bible and some pages of a favorite book. The best book for me is one about being focused and mindfully alive. I then pray in word and silence and as simply as possible. I try and sit still for a bit before heading out to run (mixed now with more walking as I age), endeavoring to keep a prayerful mind-set. I particularly value running easy and walking on remote and varied trails in woods but can make neighborhood streets work if necessary. Sometimes, I meet a good friend for all or part of the run but more so for good company, conversation, and shared silence.

After many years, I now truly enjoy and embrace my predawn time. Like everything with significance, it is a work in progress and varies in quality. Sometimes, it is almost magical. Other times, I rush through it and negate its helpfulness, fall asleep, or get distracted. When my practice grossly deteriorates or I reach a point of exhaustion, I take a break for a day or two, then crave a return to purposely starting my day. I might also change up how I go about initiating my days, reminding myself that the goal is not the ritual itself but effectual groundwork for being whole.

I always struggle to live gently and peacefully in the moment, regardless of the time of day. Yet my batting average to approach such a rich life experience goes up when I seek to follow an intentional routine of beginning and rebeginning each and every day. The "right" cluster of daily first-thing deliberate activity and inactivity is a personal matter. Although each person's search for and experience of the ideal mix will vary, the outline Jesus offers us from his effective routine long ago offers powerful tools for a more meaningful, moment-to-moment life.

Chapter 2

Simply Being Kind

In addition to the grief and sadness, funerals are often learning experiences. My father, and lifelong friend, died in February 2007 after a fierce but relatively short bout with bladder cancer. His memorial service in a small east Texas community church was part of a day to "get through." After speaking at the service and hearing the spontaneous, unexpected, beautiful tribute offered by my son, Rusty, I was spent. Then I learned something more about Dad.

As I shook hands and received hugs in an impromptu reception line after the service, I saw a man from the local grocery store, wearing his work shirt and name tag, approach me in tears. My dad was in that store all the time. So often, in fact, that we made jokes about it behind his back. What could he be doing in there? After all, a seventy-five-year-old man can only buy so many apples and so much orange juice and milk. Once a day was a light day! Our jokes stopped the day Dad left for the store, which was a mile or so from his home near Tyler, and was found disoriented in a post office parking lot in Arkansas because of cancer-induced dementia. My brother and I had been trying to wrestle the keys away from him, but he had a stubborn streak.

I did not know this man who approached me after my dad's service, but what he said through his tears made a lasting impression. "We will all miss your dad coming into the store so very much," he started. "I did not really know him, but he always spoke to me, called me by my name, asked about my day, and made me feel special—every time he was in the store." What a legacy.

What do day-to day experiences teach us about faith? The person who treats others with kindness, respect, and active caring is godly regardless of creedal affirmation or lack thereof. Dad was a Christian. He taught me Sunday school in the second grade but more so taught me by the way he treated other people, even ones he did not know. I have an even better model in retrospect as I have heard from countless people in his community who miss him.

I studied theology in graduate school and have been a student of the Bible most of my life. In my view, the Bible is a diverse and rich collection of historically inspired pieces, with the teachings of Jesus being both the heart and high point. There are more questions than answers in its pages, but the journey through religious questions and complexities leads me back to an emphasis on simplicity of action by loving and caring. The important contemporary issues that divide well-intentioned people within and across all faiths are inconsequential in comparison to the priority of how each person treats others in their respective circumstances. Spiritual authenticity is about action.

Is the Christian gospel—or the core of any legitimate faith tradition—any more complex than how one acts from day to day, especially how one treats others? Most anyone can parrot a belief, creedal formula, or opinion, but working at truly being good to others is our real calling. We question, judge, and even condemn others from different faith traditions or with a different perspective in our own congregation, community, or family, as if our litmus tests are God-given. I do not think God has any litmus test, just a common calling to serve others, to be gracious as God is gracious, whatever our circumstances.

Thank you, Dad, for showing me what is truly important, to the point that strangers remember your consistent acts of kindness.

Chapter 3

Are Questions the Answer? The Kingdom and Inquisitive Children

"Are we there yet?" Our children, Rusty and Courtney, asked that and other questions a lot as kids, especially on family trips. I thought of that recently going north on IH-35 as I do each week for my work at Baylor University in Waco, Texas. As I sleepily entered Belton, I saw it—the billboard announces that Mother Someone (let's just call her "Mama") has the answers to all of your questions. I suppose Mama patiently sits and fully answers all questions or reads palms, probably for a fee. Wow, Mama must be rich.

In matters of faith, however, are we spiritually richer with answers to hard questions or with greater inquiry? Within the Christian tradition in the concise Gospel of Mark, Jesus announces that the "kingdom of God is at hand" to start his ministry and teachings (1:15). Later, Jesus welcomes children while his adult companions try to send them off. Maybe they asked too many questions! I can imagine Jesus smiling as the queries piled up, encouraging more inquiry and maybe occasionally hinting at a response. Jesus then tells us that the kingdom of God *belongs* to such children. The key here is not to split hairs over the meaning of the kingdom but to appreciate that attention to how children think and act offers a door to God.

Kids are simple in so many model ways, especially in their attitude and activity. They (well, most of them) are loving, humble and nonjudgmental. Yet they are also incredibly inquisitive. Courtney and Rusty had never-ending questions. They were and are stellar children and adults. As kids, crisp, clear (or so I thought) answers were not enough to satisfy them. Rather, I appreciate retrospectively that their questions were formative and resulted in greater energy, exploration, and growth, both intellectually and spiritually. Importantly, unanswered questions did not hinder their practical, active expressions of love and care for others.

What does it mean to be truly childlike and thereby a kingdom person who is journeying closer to God? Some people and even faith communities utilize the “Mama approach” to God, offering answers to all of life’s questions, often in neat sound bites. Worse yet, some can be “belief police” about it, insisting that their answers are for all as a matter of life and death—and where one “goes” beyond death. The simple answer approach might be helpful for some, but I say: “No thank you, Mama.” I would rather be a child.

As our kids matured, so did their questions: If God is good, why is there injustice and seemingly arbitrary suffering in the world? That is one challenging theological question worthy of continuing reflection, but we agreed there is no simplistic, satisfying answer. There is, however, clarity in how we should *respond* to injustice and suffering. Jesus taught his followers to love their neighbor, using the time-honored parabolic example of a foreigner (Samaritan) caring for a Jewish pilgrim who had been unjustly robbed and injured on a road out of

Jerusalem (Lk 10:29–37). The Good Samaritan did not pause to discern the situation before helping. Likewise, we need not have all of our spiritual questions answered before we respond to the needs of others.

A significant common ground of great religious traditions is a call to actively love others by reaching out and meeting needs. In contrast, what divides people of faith is often a difference of theological opinion. Have you noticed, though, that children can disagree with one another but play together anyway?

"Ask and ye shall receive"—not all the answers but real community and access to God's kingdom, here and now. "Are we there yet?" No, but we are in a good, inquiring place along the path.

Chapter 4

Heaven on Earth

I turned toward my grandmother Mimmy with tears in my eight-year-old eyes, holding the simplistic religious tract and deeply afraid. Someone near an east Texas church hosting a revival had given it to me. The tract asked a question that you will probably recognize if you grew up in the South: "If you died today, would you go to heaven or hell?" Sensing my instantaneous horror as I stared at the tract's picture of literal eternal punishment for the characters lining up for the flames, Mimmy put it in the trash. Then she hugged and reassured me that God loves me each day and always will, just like her.

Although I have been spared the thumbs-up or -down afterlife picture and related graphic depiction of consequences for years, due in large part to better ecclesiastical choices, I saw it on a sign recently while driving through central Texas and gagged. The inquirer might have had good intentions, but this scare tactic "question" simply misses the mark. The attorney in me immediately wants the key terms and their context clarified. The Christian in me asks: "What about how God intends for us to live *today* and the results in *this life*?"

Regarding terminology, it seems that a fundamental assumption in the archaic question is that heaven and hell are places out (or worse yet down) there to be fully experienced after death. They are allegedly removed from our current place and time. An additional underlying component of the question appears to be that going to one place or the other is a consequence of some type of decision, affirmation, and/or conversion at a point in time. More often than not, I suspect the person asking the question probably has a blueprint for such that more than likely corresponds to what that person has confessed (or worse yet, was told to say).

Although I have a strong belief in an afterlife, the futuristic heaven or hell inquiry is disjointed. Let's be positive and focus on heaven. It is as much or more about now than the future. As Jesus taught in the Sermon on the Mount, our eye should be on today without a worry for even tomorrow (Mt 6:34). More importantly, our focus should be on our neighbors' present needs. If anyone should pose a simplistic question about heaven or hell and tomorrow, perhaps it should be the one in need asking: "If I die today because you did not help me, where might you be headed?"

We live here and now, so what does heaven have to do with us? It depends on our definition. In *Simply Christian* (Harper Collin 2006), N. T. Wright explains that heaven is God's realm while earth is mankind's realm. Heaven is not "out there" as if we could board a space shuttle and head toward it. Rather, it is very close, as if through a thin membrane. Per Wright, Jesus ushered in an overlap of heaven and earth and encouraged his followers to be part of it.

Jesus started his ministry by announcing that the kingdom of God was at hand and then showed the kingdom to us in his life and teachings. In particular, his Sermon on the Mount in Matthew 5–7 and other key teachings invite us to be God's agents here and now to continue ushering in and realizing the kingdom. This means living in God's realm—heaven—and making it happen today. Jesus is a lot more concerned about *how* people choose to live here and now than where they will "go" later. He teaches us to reach out, love, and care for others as the prescription for living in the very real intersection of heaven and earth. That is the gospel in a nutshell.

Mimmy's Christian name was Grace, as in how God relates to us and expects us to relate to one another, now and always, on earth as it is in heaven.

Chapter 5

Friendship in a Comfortless Zone

After thoroughly searching my car, the armed guard warned me: "If you try and take in any more than your one car key, a driver's license, and more than twenty dollars in quarters, you will be forced to leave." What followed was a more intrusive personal search than the "step out of the line, sir" type at the airport. I was entering a maximum security women's prison a few hours north of Austin, Texas. I neither had family there nor had I ever met anyone at the facility, prisoner or otherwise.

I not only exited my comfort zone that first day of visitation in January 2010, but I felt like I was entering the twilight zone. I walked through the heavy gates and into the prison to a large antiquated room with some tables and two uncomfortable oval areas in the middle lined with hard plastic chairs and thick Plexiglas. I would later learn that family members of prisoners could sit with them at the same table to visit, but other visitors like me sat on the plank-like chairs. We talked through scratched glass via black phones with heavy cords, overwhelmed by static for exactly two hours and not a second longer. It brought back childhood memories of the crime shows on our black-and-white TV, except instead of watching the TV set, now I was in the set.

So how did I arrive at that place? A prisoner read my article on the faith page of the Austin paper in May 2009. It was about my dad passing away and how his graceful living impacted numerous people. She wrote me a few months later at Baylor after tracking down an address. Fortunately for me, I did not immediately dismiss it as "prisoner mail," asking for legal help I was not in a position to render. Rather, I read the letter. What I discovered in its pages was sympathy for my loss and an implicit heartfelt call for communication with another person who shared her Christian faith.

After some paranoid delusion of what terrible things might result from sending a response, I recalled the parable of Jesus in Matthew 25 (vv. 31–46) of the great judgment. The scene is a cosmic throne room with people separated before the King into groups of sheep and goats based on actions (or not) taken in their lives in response to apparent needs, including hunger, thirst, illness, and incarceration. All before the judgment seat are startled to learn that the way they treated the so-called "least" of people in this life equated to the way they treated the Lord himself. The key teaching is not a prophetic "you better watch out and be good so that you can go to heaven after you die." Rather, it is a vivid first century story to drive home the truth that how we practically treat others in need is of paramount importance to our relationship with God and our own well-being.

The journey for me from writing the article about my dad to waiting to meet a prisoner included months of corresponding weekly with my new friend. She started out a complete stranger. Nevertheless, I found that I progressively anticipated receiving each letter and writing back. We were getting to know each other as we dialogued about a variety of personal and faith related issues, her from an educated and deeply Catholic perspective with key interests in spirituality and mysticism, and me from a moderate Baptist, somewhat free-thinking perspective with an east Texas twist. Our backgrounds and present circumstances differed dramatically, but I had come to treasure her pen-pal company.

As I squirmed in the uncomfortable chair awaiting my new friend's arrival that winter day, I asked myself several questions: Why was she there? What had she done? *What in the world* was I doing there on a Saturday after a hard week at work? In that moment I truly realized that for our continuing communication and blossoming friendship, it did not matter what led to her current predicament and that I was there because she had asked me to come, and I agreed. She did not need to earn or otherwise justify talking with me. Rather, I needed to continue to approach our relationship prospectively.

After waiting some thirty or more minutes, a thin woman about my age dressed in all white approached the same numbered chair opposite the heavy glass, sat down, picked up the phone, and said, "Hello and thank you so very much for coming." Two hours later, we knew each other better, and I knew I would be back once a month with quarters for cold drinks from vending machines, rarities for prisoners.

Whatever your religious orientation (or not), taking a chance to reach out to another person in need can be a wonderful way to connect and enhance, perhaps even reignite, your faith as well as your life. It can be as simple as writing a letter. There are needs all around us—pick one or allow it to pick you, then open up and embrace the blessings that flow. You may well find that you were the one in need.

CHAPTER 6

Trials on the Trails: Identity in the Wilderness

"Was it a big wolf, Gran?" asked my then three-year-old grandson Luke after I described my recent encounter on a trail run in the beautiful Forest Ridge section of the Bull Creek Greenbelt in Austin. The beast was wild and at home while I was a visitor in this treasured wilderness of sorts in the middle of our city. I go there and to the Barton Creek trails to run and walk, often getting a bit lost but finding myself in the process.

It is no surprise that the church and our country have had huge issues with the wilderness in the past. These areas untouched by humankind were places feared by the faithful and to be conquered by our predecessors in North America. While our nation by the 1960s legally embraced wilderness lands as the treasures of our federal land system to be preserved for primal escapes now and enjoyment by future generations, the church has never really been comfortable with the wilderness. After all, the children of Israel had problems there, and Jesus struggled alone with the devil.

Although our local greenbelt trail systems are not technically wilderness areas, they have the same character: pristine and undeveloped with limited access for primitive activities such as running and hiking. I love to run and have done so each morning since I was twenty years old. I was fifty, however, before I discovered the unique physical and spiritual experience of remote trail running. The surroundings are a sanctuary not only for special critters such as the wolf-like coyote at Bull Creek but also for solitary and introspective reflection.

As a Christian, I look to Jesus as a model in what he taught and how he lived. What did Jesus accomplish in the wilderness? The gospel writers tell us that Jesus heard a voice at his baptism announcing that he was God's son and was then led by the Spirit into the wilderness where he was tempted by Satan for an extended time (Mk 1:9–13). Although there is a tendency to perceive this dark struggle in negative terms, it can instead be understood as a formative and searching time. Jesus wrestled with doubts and temptations related to his identity and sense of mission so that he could understand his divine calling before actively emerging into a powerful, caring, and inclusive public ministry.

What a fine example for us. If Jesus needed to get away for intentional, prayerful self-examination, then we certainly can benefit in solitary diversion from our daily routines to thoughtfully consider our gifts, opportunities, and circumstances and reexamine the way we live each day. Actually taking the time in a special place away from the daily, rushed bombardment of noise can help us establish or get back in touch with priorities and "come out" with renewed energy to put them in action.

Jesus had some key points of reference in his quest to discern his vocation. Some circles of first century Judaism and some of those who followed and encouraged Jesus expected a militaristic messiah-type to deliver them from hated Roman dominion and occupancy and usher in God's kingdom on earth.

Questions of Jesus in the Gospels by the personified Satan, luring him to be king of the world and use his gifts for material gain and notoriety (Lk 4:1–13), perhaps reflect a temptation to be this type of powerful political and military leader. In contrast to this expectation, there was a most different model for Jesus going back hundreds of years to the time when the Jews were returning to their land from Babylonian exile: a humble, suffering servant of God figure reflected in the middle and latter portions of the book of Isaiah. Jesus embraced this model to enlighten what it meant to be God's special child. Luke tells us in his Gospel that Jesus went straight to the synagogue in his hometown after returning from the wilderness. He read from Isaiah, indicating that the Spirit was upon him to "bring good news to the poor" and set the oppressed free, which he proceeded to do (Lk 4:14–22).

Most of us have meaningful points of reference that we can take into the woods as tools for examining our talents and auditing how we are living, including from faith traditions, respected friends and teachers, and influential role models. Using our gifts to actively care for those in our trust and others in need is a stellar beginning for a response action plan when we return.

Chapter 7

Feeling Fear but Not Being Afraid

"Dad, please don't let go yet!" I screamed at age five before realizing that my dad indeed had already taken his hands off the back of my first bicycle. One moment I was riding all by myself and the next I was in a neighbor's yard after crashing into the curb.

"You did it, Son! Let's get up now and do it again." I felt scared, overwhelmed with fear, but Dad encouraged me not to be afraid of trying it again. Mired in my fearful emotion, I would never have moved ahead with the process toward such an enjoyable activity.

There is a marked difference between feeling fear and choosing to be afraid. In the first chapter of his insightful book *Conquering Fear* (Random House 2009), Harold Kushner asserts that God's injunction not to be afraid occurs over eighty times in the Bible, leading Rabbi Kushner to suggest an eleventh commandment: "Do not be afraid." In the Christian Scriptures, Jesus often tells his followers the same. God himself affirms in one striking example where Jesus is "transfigured" and covered by a cloud, telling a select group of apostles who accompanied Jesus to "listen" to his special son (Mk 9:2, 7). It is reasonable to assume that whatever the nature of this mountaintop experience, these men must have been trembling with fear. Luke tells us they were terrified (Lk 9:34). Matthew describes them as "overcome by fear," but Jesus assured them, "[D]o not be afraid" (Mt 17:6–7). God was not alarmed at the instinctively normal human sensation of fear; rather, he wanted the disciples to listen and put the teachings of Jesus into action and not remain petrified.

Looking back on my childhood, I was glad my dad taught me to ride a bike but ashamed with my reaction to my mother's best efforts for me to learn to play the piano. I took lessons for a few months from a gifted teacher and even played "Ride the Train" (challenging for me at the time) at the Woman's Building in Tyler in front of a lot of other kids' moms. I was afraid of the hard work and potential failure associated with persevering, so I made numerous whining excuses and quit even though Mom was ready to help me.

Although fear often plays an essential role in our lives, such as warning us to avoid a fire or walk across an interstate, it can have a paralyzing effect in worthwhile endeavors, such as riding a bike, playing the piano, or more importantly, endeavoring to live a godly life. Jesus set tough, qualitative standards in the Sermon on the Mount (Mt 5–7) for living a Christian life. The opening of this collection of sayings in Matthew 5 includes a series of beatitudes, indicating for example that the "merciful," "pure in heart," and "peacemakers" are blessed (vv. 7–9). Seeking to live a life of pure intention full of merciful acts and works toward peace invites vulnerability and potential failure. Apprehension is expected, but being afraid is a chosen state of hesitancy to avoid trying. The same is true of any other religious or vocational calling, utilization of talents, or pursuit of a worthwhile objective. As Kushner suggests, "Our goal should not be the total absence of fear but the mastery of fear" so that it does not "keep us from doing the things we yearn to do."

When I was fourteen years old, my dad came home one day and found me sitting on the curb near our home with a neighbor. I was bleeding, missing several teeth, and too dizzy to stand up moments after a bad bike wreck where I planted my face and chin on the pavement of a big hill. My father wrapped his strong arms around me and held my hand for several hours in the ER and in the dreadful dentist's chair. Many months and nightmares later, and with Dad by my side, although trembling, I started to ride my bike again.

God walks with us in our pursuit of righteousness, utilization of gifts, and meaningful aspirations. In the well-known Psalm 23, the pilgrim is comforted walking through the valley of the shadow of death or "darkest valley" by God's companionship as a shepherd (Ps 23:4). When we fall off of our intended path of how to live, maximize our talents, or realize our dreams, God can pick us up and redirect us through the gauntlet of our fears, often through those we love. When we see others stall along their path, let us offer assistance to be God's hand to encourage and help them continue on their journey.

CHAPTER 8

Image or Action?

Who are these people? I thought defensively as I sat alone in a crowded visitation room waiting for a friend. It was the one Sunday a month when I teach Sunday school, and I'm usually wearing running shoes and jeans before heading north. The world seems so bright and open on these days until I turn west off of IH-35 at Temple, when everything progressively narrows and darkens en route to a maximum security prison. After enduring the high-level security searches and questioning to get in, I anticipate the arrival of my friend on the other side of thick Plexiglas for our two hour visit. We each value the consistent communication weekly by mail and monthly at the prison.

When I enter the prison "zone" each month, no one cares who I think I am or how much money I make, my level of education, what I do for a living, or my personal best in the marathon. They could certainly care less if I declare, as I too often am inclined to do, that "I am a moderate, true historic Baptist" in a merciless effort to set myself apart from other "types" of Baptists and other Christian groups.

I have been going to this prison long enough to see familiar faces among other visitors, including many from diverse churches and other faith-based organizations. I expect we must have very different views on a host of religious and contemporary issues. We smile at each other and occasionally speak, saying, "Have a good visit," or "Be careful going home." We have no interest in theological squabbles or making sure the other knows our religious badge. Rather, our kinship is rooted in imperfect yet similar efforts in a sometimes uncomfortable setting to reach out to prisoners—one at a time—who simply want to talk meaningfully with another person not wearing a uniform. As I continue to look around the visitation area, I realize our common mission work is what is important, not the sometimes competitive vocalization of fundamentalist-to-liberal faith identities.

As I leave the prison late in the afternoon to reenter what feels more like my life, I wonder more particularly about divisions in my own faith tradition. Why do we care so much about our image and invest so much energy tagging ourselves publicly? Sometimes we insistently announce our identity to make sure others know who we are, and seemingly more importantly, who we are not: them!

The New Testament provides helpful information and counsel about early Christian factions with unshakable differences of opinion. For example, Paul implores Christian cliques in his letter to the Romans to prioritize love (Rom 14). These groups had divided over issues such as dietary restrictions and the observance of special days. Apparently, one group claimed to be strong, while the others insisted their opponents had no scruples. Paul (and I suspect God himself) cared more about how they treated each other than who might have the "right" opinion, as if there was one.

Paul nails authentic Christian identity in his letter to the Philippians: "Let your gentleness be known to everyone—" as in, let it be evident in how you live (Phil 4:5). In Christian terms, that is living the gospel. Paul also says not to worry about anything (v. 6). Have you ever noticed the guarded sense of anxiety and preoccupation accompanying bold assertions of religious affiliation?

Paul points to Jesus as the model for love, care, and service with humility, practically, and each and every day (2:5–11). This true gospel is easy to understand but difficult and costly to implement, in part because it is hard simply to walk and not talk. The first chapter of Mark, the earliest Gospel, provides an instructive glimpse into the daily life of Jesus. He taught, touched, and healed the sick and outcast and sought solitude for prayer and reflection. What he did not seek was attention.

We live in a culture—churches included—that emphasizes distinctive personal branding. Although spiritual identity through a contemplative process is an important part of any faith journey, immersion in advertising us and our beliefs can stifle true ministry. Practical service to others, not verbal articulation, is the superlative expression of effective faith.

Chapter 9

Mary's Close Encounter—A Model Prayer for All Seasons

On the January side of the great divide between the holiday season and New Year's Day, Christmas is in the rearview mirror and essentially "put away" until next year. Before it fades from view, however, a closer look can transform our new year with helpful resolutions, such as embarking on a fresh approach to prayer.

Experiencing true and meaningful contemplative prayer is challenging, especially in our distraction-filled cultural experience of Christmas and the exhaustion that follows. The rushed petitionary kind of prayer—such as, "Please give me this"—comes pretty easy most any time of year and especially when advertisers encourage asking for exactly what one wants. Indeed, throughout all busy seasons of life, prayer on the run fits right in if it is crammed into schedules at all.

For those who seek God in solitude and silence, there are struggles with what to say, whether one should feel anything, and how to slow down, be still, and listen. A systematic approach might help, but where can one look to keep it simple?

"The Lord is with you. . . . Do not be afraid, Mary, for you have found favor with God. . . . Here am I, the servant of the Lord"

(Lk 1:28, 30, 38). These are familiar words for Christians each holiday season from the Gospel of Luke's narrative of the angel Gabriel appearing to Mary and Mary's response.

Growing up an east Texas Protestant, I was never quite sure what to do with Mary. Jesus was center stage year-round. Mary was one of a host of supporting characters in Christmas pageants put on by children alongside Joseph and a donkey. Of course, I was always fascinated with the donkey. At some point as an adolescent in the pews, however, it occurred to me that churches like ours did way too little with Mary. Were we afraid of putting her on a pedestal? Was it some kind of gender-phobia or perhaps some apprehension of looking Catholic? Well, it just so happened that half of my family *was* Catholic.

Not surprisingly, over time I developed kind of a "Mary neurosis." Fortunately, I was encouraged from less troubled souls to be open to other traditions. I broadened my horizon and acquired a strong taste for Catholic writers such as Thomas Merton. I truly warmed up to Mary. Although ambiguities about her linger, they are unimportant to me. I realize at a minimum that Mary is a wonderful scriptural role model. Whether one worships her or not, one should seriously consider emulating her.

Mary's humble encounter with Gabriel provides an artistic blueprint for prayer throughout the year for Christians of all stripes and persons in most any faith tradition. Taking a cue from Mary coupled with imagination, consider finding a quiet, dark, familiar space to relax and breathe easy. Imagine a warm, soft greeting from God with the assurance that he truly is and always will be with us. If you prefer more of an arms-length transaction, then substitute an angel or other agent, such as a close or cherished mentor, welcoming you on God's behalf. Envision being washed of all fear and hesitation as God tells you—as he told so many in biblical accounts—not to be afraid because he loves you and favors you individually. It might be perplexing to consider all of this but no less so than for the young girl, Mary, who was given the unexpected news that she was pregnant with a unique child. Like Mary, we can choose to soak ourselves humbly in any experience even as we ponder its full meaning.

As our imagination blends into reality, we can emerge and join Mary in gratitude by responding in loving service to others. As we continue into a new year, next stage of life, or simply the next day, may we truly remember and move forward with thanksgiving and the entirety of the holiday or other meaningful experience in perspective, enabled to reach out and care for others now and always.

Chapter 10

More Than a Brother

"Son, I'm leaving home tomorrow." Gulp. The Coke my dad offered me in his Tyler insurance office that Saturday afternoon long ago suddenly tasted different, a palatable remembrance of this before and after kind of day in my life. I was seventeen years old. However, I was much younger emotionally after growing up to that point in what I sensed was an idyllic family setting. Immediate family as I knew it was breaking, but an unexpected strong bond would soon emerge.

What does it mean truly to be a brother or sister to someone? It means to be a friend in an uncommonly close sense. Indeed, it can be akin to being the hand of God. In the imagery of Psalm 23, a bona fide sibling is willing to walk with one through the valley of deepest darkness without feeling a hint of extra weight. Although it does not require a blood relationship, when there is one as I found out long ago, the brother/sisterhood connection is especially profound.

The before-my-dad-visit period of my family life was one of peace. Little did I know it was too good to be true. On that surprising day in 1973, I was playing and practicing golf as I had almost every day since Dad taught me to play in the fifth grade. I was a senior in high school with a soon-to-be-spoiled ambition to play golf seriously through college. On that seemingly pleasant fall afternoon, I had just walked the fairways and felt so relaxed. When I finished, I had a message in the golf shop (no cell phones back then) to drop by and see my dad on the way home. I walked into his familiar office and said, "What's up, Dad?" More than I knew.

The next day was a blur that I wish I could forget. My dad appeared in the living room with a suitcase. My mother sat quietly in her chair, probably unaware of what was about to happen. I knew what was coming and just wanted to hide. After getting my older brother on the phone from his University of Texas dorm room, Dad announced that he was leaving our home. Mom looked so alone, thinner than normal and with a devastated sense about her. I was shaken and felt light-years from the prior afternoon of tranquility on the links, with a new and uncertain future before me.

Among the things that stick out in retrospect from that fractured morning long ago is my brother asking to talk with me. I held the phone with a shaking hand as my brother said, "I love you." Oh, how I needed those unexpected words of comfort and support at that very moment. Yet was he the same two-and-a-half-year older brother who most of my life to that point reveled in making fun of me with nicknames like "Walrus" and "Piglet"? He was quite popular, an extrovert, played football, and always had a girlfriend. I was a recluse of sorts, introverted, lived at the golf course, and finally at age seventeen had a girlfriend. Some questioned, and still do, whether we came from the same loins!

As it turns out, that profoundly sad day in my life had a very bright spot. It marked a transition and point of progression toward a lifetime of the absolute best of both friendship and brotherhood. When I was weak, my brother was strong for me. When I wanted to stop, he picked me up and walked with me. He did not need to say, “I’m your brother,” because he just lived and continues to live it.

That dark day when Dad left home ended with me feeling lost and afraid. I did not know how to help myself or my mother. Nevertheless, I knew that I was not alone in my grief. I asked God for help. He came to me in my brother.

We might not fully appreciate how God answers prayers and meets needs, but when we see another person who is hurting, we can reach out and be a sister or brother, for a moment or a lifetime. In so doing, we take the mystery out of how God responds by taking it upon ourselves to answer the call.

Chapter 11

Canine Wisdom

"No, drop that sock right now!" I screamed. It had been a long day at work for me, but Copper spent his entire day waiting for me to come home and play with him. In response to my tone, he cowered and circled the floor with his tail tucked between his legs. I felt terrible and even closer to the ground than my faithful dachshund. I had my damp, incisor-marked sock back but no mulligan for my outburst and Copper's hurt feelings.

Dog lovers understand canine hypersensitivity to their people and speech. Although dogs might not comprehend words, they certainly react to inflection and loudness as well as our moods. Thus, we learn to be guarded when we speak to our beloved four-legged friends. What about our level of care with speech in interpersonal relationships and communications where words are also understood?

As I sat with Copper in my lap later that evening, thankful that dogs have short memories and are quick to forgive, I thought about my words that day to others: my wife, children, running buddies, colleagues at work, people who did work for me, acquaintances, and even strangers. Had I been too quick to speak or respond? From the YMCA to the running trail, then the office and meetings, off to lunch, working closely with assistants in the afternoon, and back home in the evening: Had

I used my words for harm or help, to tear down or build up? Further, why was I just now thinking about it instead of exercising patience and reflection before opening my mouth?

In the Epistle of James, the New Testament author focused on the power of the tongue: "With it we bless the Lord and Father, and with it we curse those who are made in the likeness of God. From the same mouth come blessing and cursing. My brothers and sisters, this ought not to be so" (3:9–10). Hundreds of years earlier, the writer of Proverbs similarly observed that a "gentle tongue is a tree of life, but perverseness in it breaks the spirit" (Prv 15:4).

The contemporary tongue is multifaceted and often leaves a permanent imprint. People speak literally with their tongues as well as pencil and pen. In our culture now, however, people often talk frantically with fingers and thumbs within a variety of modern and developing communicative media. From watching people more skilled than me with modern conversational devices such as smartphones, it appears the premium is often on speed and quantity of speech as opposed to reflective patience and quality of expression.

If I texted Copper and handed him my phone, he would enjoy smelling and licking it before putting it in his mouth regardless of the content. When I look into his eyes before opening my mouth, however, I remember how my words and attitude can either sting or affirm. I then more fully appreciate the premium of thinking before either opening my mouth or deciding to keep it shut. More significantly, I should pause and reflect before speaking in any way to a sister or brother. It is difficult to think about the impact of what one might say while in a hurry to talk, especially in a multitasking mode. Like the actual mouth, thumbs can be vehicles to bless or curse in an instant but with the potential for lasting consequence.

After his caution about using the tongue, the author of James describes true wisdom as "first pure, then peaceable, gentle, willing to yield, full of mercy and good fruits, without a trace of partiality or hypocrisy" (Jas 3:17). What a beautiful model for living a "good life" (v. 13), including as a standard to be wise in all speech.

My dog Copper has taught me a lot in his short life. He "speaks" to me gently with his eyes and a touch of his snout and enthusiastically with a wagging tail, all without any words. What instructive, counterculture wisdom. Often it is best just to be quiet and simply touch others with kind actions.

Chapter 12

Principled but without Scruples

Someone very close to me needed a Good Samaritan recently. During her daily power walk, she tripped and fell in the street near her home. Unfortunately, the only passerby was another walker who must have seen her hit the pavement but failed to ask if she was hurt or even acknowledge her existence. He actually lived down the street (a neighbor in appearance only). The man (not to be confused with a gentleman) was known in the neighborhood as a scrupulous participant in an extremist sect of his mainline religion. One apparent tenet he followed was avoidance of women, including in conversation and perhaps more so if they did not share his faith tradition. I wonder if it brought him closer to God or provided a sense of spiritual fulfillment to "stay strong" and not touch her hand to help her up or speak and ask if she needed help.

About a mile from the very spot of this incident, many years ago, I was running in a 5K race; back then I was locally competitive in my age group (or maybe just in my own mind). Wheelchair participants started this relatively small race about five minutes early. I was in fifth place and moving up in a cluster of runners halfway up a long hill midway through the race. As we approached a wheelchair racer, his chair hit an obstacle. He fell out into the street about fifty yards in front of us. Although he appeared not to be seriously hurt and waved us on, I watched incredulously as all other runners, but one, simply ran by. I like to give people the benefit of the doubt, so maybe they had eyes in the back of their heads and saw the policeman riding up from behind to assist. I followed the sole role model and stopped to help, then almost killed myself after joining back in the race to pass and beat some of the others who ran by in such unprincipled fashion! I wondered if they set a personal best and met their goals that day, and if so, whether it was worth it when they looked in the mirror the next day.

People of faith and runners are sensitive, empathetic folks in my experience. The aberrations noted above glaringly demonstrate how hyper-attention to ritual or relentlessly pushing toward personal goals can stab at the true heart of legitimate faith. Central to Christianity and with roots in Judaism is the principle of prioritizing love by living it out practically and day-to-day. The "Bad Samaritan" in my friend's neighborhood and the "somebody else will surely help racers" call to mind a parable Jesus told about a very good person who loved others as he did himself. Recorded in Lk 10:29–37, Jesus told the story at a time long ago when my friend's neighbor might have been more at home! The four main characters in the story all traveled the same road from Jerusalem to Jericho: a Jewish pilgrim, beaten and left to die, and three passersby. The first two walked on by on the other side of the road while the third stopped to help with his hands that day and his money to insure follow-up care.

Like any good parable, the pilgrimage circumstances were familiar to rabbis and listeners. The first two men were Jewish like the wounded traveler, whereas the one who stopped to help was a Samaritan, a hated foreigner. Let's imagine why the two countrymen might have passed by the one in need. Were they afraid of being robbed and beaten themselves if they tarried? Perhaps there were more important things to attend to in their faith, such as avoiding potential contact with an apparent corpse to stay ritually pure. Maybe they were in a hurry for an appointment with God as the objective of an insular faith journey—important business that could not be interrupted. Could it have been as uncomplicated as them realizing they could not help everyone in distress?

The Good Samaritan was different. He saw a person in need, focused on the moment, and acted. He simply loved his neighbor and had a broad definition of the term. What an example. Reaching out to help should be unconditional and without filtering a response through a creed, balking because of scruples dressed up as faith, or exercising exclusivity. We might be afraid, like the Samaritan understandably would have been afraid on the dangerous road. Nevertheless, fear did not keep him from reaching out to another in need.

There was an overwhelming amount of hurt in the time of Jesus, just as in our time. Like Jesus in his own life, without being stifled by the multiplicity of need, we can make choices along our roads to reach out qualitatively to others one at a time.

Chapter 13

Who Is Truly Christian?

At my father's memorial service years ago, several people in his church commented: "Your dad was a good Christian." I was certainly not in an analytical mood at the time of Dad's service, but I ponder the meaning now. I have no doubt that Dad's friends intended to compliment my father and comfort me in my grief. As I reflect on the statement now, however, I wonder what the parishioners meant. Was it commentary on professed belief, a life well-lived, or both? This inquiry is relevant to authenticity in any religious faith.

More recently, a friend described a family member to me and said she was worried because "he is not a Christian" and hoped he would become one "before it is too late." Nevertheless, her description of her only son was of a selfless, overly compassionate person consistently involved day-to-day in helping others in need. I sought to reassure her that her son sounded like a saint and certainly seemed to be on the right path.

The author of the New Testament book of Acts informs us in chapter 11 that "it was in Antioch that the disciples were first called Christians" (v. 26). Thus, it appears the term "Christian" in usage was initially attached to disciples: those seeking to follow the teachings of Jesus. What about today?

People sometimes describe others as "Christian" or "not Christian," assuming the meaning is apparent. Using this term as a noun often appears linked to profession of belief. Has the other person said the appropriate faith-related words or expressed the correct opinion? This approach can be exclusivist and divisive. Distasteful examples abound in political sound bites, where opinions in a vacuum on issues such as school prayer and abortion provide neat distinctions for godliness or not. In contrast, when the word "Christian" is used more in an adjectival sense to describe loving and caring activity, it can have a more affirming, inclusive, and accurate sense.

What did Jesus historically have in mind when he said "follow me" as he did so often—creed or behavior? More often than not, I believe that Jesus called for response—*action* to his teaching instead of words or otherwise putting on some kind of show for others.

Perhaps the best scriptural source of the teachings of Jesus is the Sermon on the Mount in chapters 5–7 of the Gospel of Matthew. Jesus denounced hypocrites who sounded a trumpet in giving to the poor, prayed loudly on the street corners, and made a public display of suffering when they fasted. Instead, Jesus encouraged giving alms in secret, praying simply with few words in private, and being content with only God witnessing a religious rite such as fasting (6:1–18).

Later in this discourse, Jesus articulated what we call the Golden Rule: "In everything do to others as you would have them do to you" (7:12). Discipleship in action is the "narrow" gate and the hard road noted in the next few verses that leads to abundant life here and now. It is the *doing* that matters. The opposite? "Force others to parrot belief identical to yours and express correct opinions like yours or be damned." Indeed,

Jesus specifically denounced judgment of others in this same sermon (vv. 1–5).

At the close of his teaching in the Sermon on the Mount, Jesus described a wise and a foolish person in terms of whether each actually responds to his teachings. Those who hear and act on his words are founded on rock, whereas others who hear and fail to act have no true grounding (vv. 24–27). So, as a famous NBA player once asked in a press conference: "Are you talking about practice?" Yes, it is the practice that counts as "Christian" and not words or stage performance for others.

Chapter 14

The Importance of 2012 (or Any Other Time)

Do you recall the apocalyptic interest in 2012? I am not an "end of the world is a coming" kind of guy, but I did agree with Mayan calendar enthusiasts that the year 2012 was of utmost importance at the time. I disagreed, however, that the winter solstice (December 21, 2012) was the most important day on the calendar. The most important day of 2012 and of any other year is in fact today—and we should be ever mindful of it.

I admit I have never examined any end of time predictions related to the Mayas or otherwise. This will probably not change, but my non-job-related reading list has expanded a bit in the last few years. The bookshelves in my study at home are dominated by exercise and Christian theology (non-Armageddon-type) books with very little in between. Recently after digesting Larry Shapiro's delightful book *Zen and the Art of Running* (Adams Media 2009), however, I stretched at the invitation of my daughter Courtney and read several books by Thich Nhat Hanh. Brother Hanh helped open me to the concept of mindfulness: being fully aware, attentive, and responsive to the day, the very moment, at hand. He also reminded me that in my own tradition this principle is central in the life and teachings of Jesus.

In a nutshell, Brother Hanh is a Vietnamese Buddhist monk. His history of strong, nonviolent advocacy for peace earned him a Nobel Peace Prize nomination by Martin Luther King Jr. in the 1960s as well as a passionate plea by Father Thomas Merton for his safety in the context of personal threats in his homeland. Hanh is a prolific writer. His words and approach to life are clear and simple. Hanh also refreshingly finds common ground with other religions, mine included, by emphasizing the practice of faith over the articulation of it. For example, he draws a number of parallels between the life and teachings of Jesus and Buddha in his *Living Buddha, Living Christ* (Riverhead Books 2007). Hahn's loving approach to embracing the best of non-Buddhist traditions is a welcome and instructive perspective compared with the more common guarded and defensive "mine is authentic and yours is not" attitude. Similar to Hanh, but within the Catholic tradition, Merton embraced parallels with other religious traditions and encouraged proactive interfaith dialogue. The ecumenically minded Merton fondly referred to Hanh as his "brother."

Hanh's ideas opened me to a fresh understanding of the core of my own faith in considering what it means to follow the example of Jesus. Jesus lived a life of quintessential mindfulness. Crowds gathered around him with a proliferation of needs. Instead of being overwhelmed by the multitudes and the limitations imposed by humanity, Jesus met the needs of others in service one at a time as they presented themselves to him and without any rush. I picture Jesus stopping to slow down on his journey day-to-day, attentive to and focused upon the person before him.

Enemies of mindfulness include obsessive attachment to the past and dreaming of the future. Both involve a preoccupation that detracts from being fully present right now. Jesus gave many people comfort in their lives to forget the past and move forward. A prime example is his response to the woman caught in adultery in John 8. Certain leaders quizzed Jesus about whether to kill her by casting stones per their narrow, unrelenting, and literal reading and application of historic Jewish law. Jesus responded by suggesting anyone free of wrongdoing throw the first rock. After the frenzied crowd settled down and disbursed, Jesus set the woman free without condemnation and told her to go her way without sin "from now on" (Jn 8:11). Regarding the future, Jesus taught his disciples in the Sermon on the Mount in Matthew 6 not to worry about their lives and in particular not to fret about tomorrow (v. 34). Rather, the proper and healthy focal point is today.

When followers of Jesus asked him for signs and about the timing of future events in Mark 13, he told them neither he nor the angels in heaven knew (v. 32). Actually, Jesus had already told them where to concentrate their attention. At the beginning of his public ministry in 1:15, Jesus announced what time it was for his and our generation: "The time is fulfilled, and the kingdom of God is at hand." The time is now and always will be.

Chapter 15

Season of Choice

In one ear I heard gentle, empathetic offers to help me in a difficult time of transition, but in the other, harsh directives that it was my "responsibility to get my parents back together." Such was my worst holiday season ever. I handled it poorly. I retreated, including from those reaching out in love. I was miserable. It was Christmas 1973, my first after my parents' unexpected split that fractured the warm, secure home I had known all my life to that point. As an immature and shaken seventeen-year-old, I chose to withdraw that holiday. I spent as much of the season as possible alone on a remote golf course while others seemed to join happily with their family and friends. If there had been ready access to a cave, I suppose I would have used it as my Christmas dwelling.

Several years of healing later, while in graduate school, I read Viktor Frankl's *From Death Camp to Existentialism*. This book is typically found today under the less captivating title *Man's Search for Meaning* (Beacon Press 1959). I was initially introduced to Frankl in my Psychology of Religion class. My professor characterized him as the founder of the Third Viennese School of Psychotherapy. (Whatever that means.) Instead of focusing on what seemed to me stale comparisons to Freud and Adler, I took Frankl's book to heart. It has been part of my life ever since. I read it every year and embrace this holiday tradition of reading and rereading a truly meaningful book. It always encourages me to make better attitudinal choices and respond in a healthier manner to all of life's circumstances, including the most difficult ones.

Frankl's central idea is simple and profound but not always easy to implement: Whatever our circumstances, we are free to choose our attitude and response. Although events and other people can hurt and even devastate us, we make our own choice of perspective. According to Frankl in *Man's Search for Meaning*: "Everything can be taken from a man or woman but one thing: the last of human freedoms, to choose one's attitude in any given set of circumstances, to choose one's way." Many of us would bristle at this suggestion because no one has known our particular pain and the related severity of our problems. To borrow a legal concept, however, Frankl has "standing" to comment on positive attitudinal election. He survived Auschwitz. His own death camp experiences and observations of others formed the basis of his ideas and suggestions.

Frankl's Holocaust account is unique because he focuses on stories of personal reaction and related survival efforts as opposed to cataloging details of atrocities. Kushner observes in comments on the book that "Frankl's concern is less with the question of why most died than it is with the question of why anyone at all survived." Kushner then focuses on one of Frankl's key ideas: "Life is not primarily a quest for pleasure . . . or a quest for power . . . but a quest for meaning." Similar to Frankl, Kushner's life observations are worthy of our attention. His *When Bad Things Happen to Good People* (Random House 1981) was the result of his son's serious illness and all too brief life. In this and other works, Kushner consistently highlights the importance of how people respond to challenging situations and sees God present in their gentle, loving, caring, and gracious response action.

In a moving passage from his book, *Man's Search for Meaning*, Frankl recalls how vivid mental images of his wife helped him cope with and escape from day-to-day difficulties. He did not know where she was or her fate, but thoughts of her made her "more luminous than the sun" and helped him conclude that the "salvation of man is through love and in love."

I have had a fortunate and charmed life in so many ways. People who truly love and care for me, especially my wife, children, grandchildren, brother, and close friends, surround and support me. Although my challenges in life pale relative to those of others, I have my own dark places and deep wounds. Those stemming from an unexpected broken home many years ago still sting. With God's help through others, however, I endeavor to choose an attitude and a way with true meaning. Reading Frankl's masterpiece annually helps me make better choices and wakes me up to real priorities in my life with a fresh new year in sight.

Years ago I told a Christian friend that two of my favorite authors were Frankl and Kushner. He was surprised: "Why are Jewish writers your favorite?" I gave a nice, lame response while thinking his question was odd. After all, we as Christians endeavor to live in a manner worthy of the teachings and life model of a Jewish rabbi who pointed to God as love in all seasons and for all people.

Chapter 16

All God's Children

A few years ago, as our then five-year-old grandson Luke pulled down the shirt collar of his six-week-old cousin Chuck, he asked: "Is he that color all over or just on his face?" All over. The ever curious and inquisitive Luke, however, was just getting started. "Will he always be the same color?" "Do people ever change colors?"

My wife and I are blessed with a beautiful, loving, and diverse family. Joyously, we all reside in Austin. Three of our five grandchildren, Luke, little brother Brady, and littler sister Sadie are Caucasian. Their cousin Chuck is African American. Chuck's older sister Bell is part African American and part Caucasian via eastern Europe. Color differences are fascinating among these precious siblings and cousins, purely incidental to their close relationships with one another.

Turning the clock back to when I grew up in Tyler in the 1960s, skin color was an unfortunate gateway for relationships or the lack thereof. In that era, color, faith choices, and other differences were often cause for judgment instead of innocent curiosity. Unfortunately, things have not changed much in some circles today, including the uncalled-for violent manifestations of hatred. Indeed, one act of terror or violence would be too many.

The early 1970s in east Texas and elsewhere was a tense time of forced desegregation but de facto segregation. I graduated from high school in 1974, three years after integration and the unfortunate riots and police patrolled campus that accompanied it. Bladder infections were frequent as campus bathrooms were more fighting than biological relief stations. Oftentimes, the fighters were people of all colors who came from off campus to stir up trouble.

I escaped from those racially intense high school years to the University of Texas, but I spent my first two summers back in Tyler in what would become my best work and ethnic experience ever. I worked at Lake Tyler on a crew that took care of six large, developed properties. We worked hard and did everything from housework to yard work to taking a massive amount of trash to the city dump every Monday. We were a crew of five: one main boss, two full-time employees, and two summer workers. I was the only white guy. The others, my boss James included, were black.

At the start of my first summer at Lake Tyler, I was uneasy because of lingering high school memories. The circumstances were so new and different for me. Unlike my brother and many friends from high school who played football and had opportunities to interact positively and cooperatively in racially diverse settings, I played high school golf on an all-white team. Thus, that summer job was my first truly consistent, diverse encounter. It was also a first-time experience of being in the minority five days a week for three months. I was nervous and must admit a bit afraid. Less than three years later, however, James was an honored guest at my wedding. I will never forget the pure sense of joy I felt when I greeted James that day and received a treasured bear hug.

In the interim during those formative summers, my new friends sensed and quickly calmed my fears as they treated me like their brother. We worked hard and had fun together. We watched out for each other during dangerous tasks. We also sometimes talked about important issues, but mostly we simply worked together to repair and clean things up.

During those two summers when I was age nineteen and twenty, I learned a lot in a short time about what is really important in life. I learned not to be color-blind but color appreciative. That work crew experience was one of bonding and the imparting of wisdom by example. It was wisdom from a different culture to complement lessons of love and inclusiveness my parents and church mentors taught me. Now I had the missing piece beyond important words: experience. It was and is a "wisdom from above" as the author of the New Testament book of James calls it, "without a trace of partiality or hypocrisy" (3:17). I will never forget those fine men. Their positive footprints in my past continually inform my life.

Similar to other children of varying heritage, our grandchildren play and interact with each other with graceful ease, highlighting and celebrating differences that unite all into a whole. When they do not understand something that is different, they calmly ask questions, then listen and learn. Jesus taught us to welcome children and that the kingdom of God belongs to them and to those who become childlike. When we need a reminder of how to live and embrace others, the playground at a diverse local park might be a good place to sit and observe for a while.

CHAPTER 17

Trust the Person, Not the Label

"She's a criminal!" Such was the harsh comment and intended conclusive description of my new friend after I described our recent visits to an acquaintance. Unlike this self-righteous confident observer, however, I actually knew her personally as a fine and model individual locked in a current set of unfortunate circumstances. Regardless of her past and why she was incarcerated, my friend dealt quite well with *how* not only to survive but truly live in a rough environment. Thus, I found the stereotyping and inability to see beyond the "criminal" classification revolting. I thought disdainfully of the accuser: "What a myopic jerk." I realized my hypocrisy, however, because I might have rushed to the same dismissive conclusion about my friend before I really got to know her.

Classifying people is unavoidable in our culture. Groupings in some circumstances are helpful and even protective. Labels can also serve an introductory role, such as, "She's a runner," or "He's a teacher." Interestingly, people often prefer to introduce or identify themselves with reference to one or more groups, using the tags like brand names of sorts. Unfortunately, however, branding others can also be used to stigmatize them. The practice sometimes reeks of condemnation and discrimination, including in religious settings. Characterizing someone in a harsh tone as a "conservative," "zealot" or "liberal" typically is not a sign of endearment or wanting to spend quality time together.

At a minimum, group characterizations such as these can inhibit meaningful dialogue and true relationships.

The Faith Club by Ranya Idliby, Suzanne Oliver, and Pricilla Warner (Simon and Schuster 2006) is a beautiful and refreshing autobiographic account of open and respectful communication between a Jew, Muslim, and Christian. The three authors are all mothers of small children in post-9/11 New York City. Theirs is a compelling story of courage, self-examination, and growth. It is a model for constructive interfaith and intra-faith dialogue.

One especially telling section of the book is Chapter Five, entitled, “Stop Stereotyping Me!” The women each wrestle honestly and courageously with their preconceived images of the other two. At the outset, instead of unique individuals, they are instead respectively “Christian,” “Muslim,” and “Jew” accompanied by certain negative and unfair culturally induced images. Further, each woman realizes to some extent self-conscious attempts to avoid being victimized by imagined stereotypical judgment of the others. One of my favorite, watershed-type lines in *The Faith Club* is when Oliver says, “Now it was time to take off our uniforms and begin talking about the real people underneath.” It was true of how they viewed one another as well as themselves. As a result of their deliberate interaction, the authors end up becoming true and supportive friends with an authentic, real-life appreciation of their own and other religious traditions.

I have been writing my so-called criminal friend for several years. I also visit her periodically at the prison. She is a model

Christian in many ways. She is humble, thankful, and kind. She listens more than she talks. She has more genuine and caring interest for me than many people I have known in my life. Although she does not understand a lot of what has happened to her and she lives in a very challenging setting, my friend does not appear bitter. She often thanks me for my time and friendship, but I am the primary recipient of God's grace through her.

Before my friend initially wrote me a letter, we did not know anything about each other. I worked though false perceptions and images, as I expect she did about me. Essentially, I was afraid of moving ahead with communication, and later, after months of writing, I feared even more going to the prison to visit with her. Fear drives and more so inhibits so much in life, including the negative use of labels for people and failure to work beyond them to really see the person.

Christian and Jewish scriptures are full of the admonition: "Do not be afraid." As we encounter others who seem different or foreign to us, if we sense these gentle words to relax and open ourselves a bit, we might well encounter unexpected blessings and end up understanding and bettering ourselves in the process.

Chapter 18

Footprints, Choices, and the Path Ahead

On a crisp recent morning as I sat on my porch with the sun rising, a cup of coffee in my hand, and my dog in my lap, I smiled as I noticed the small handprint in the concrete near my foot. Part of the porch slab was poured years ago before our grandson Luke turned two. I remember like it was yesterday, his dad (our son Rusty) placing Luke's hand in the wet concrete mix to leave an indelible mark. Luke's hand is much bigger now. He also does not need any help using it.

Looking back at my foot during the idyllic start of that peaceful day, I remembered my own small footprints on the beach as a child while on a family vacation to the Gulf Coast. I walked along the wet sand at the water's edge with my dad. I repeatedly looked back to watch the gentle waves roll away any trace of my footprints. As I moved ahead, I twisted my route from time to time in anticipation of my temporary marks being washed away out the back.

We can learn so much being attentive to children and contemplating our own childhood. Similar to my grandson's mark on the floor, our actions and words in life create a permanent monument of sorts that is our past. Yet, like my walk long ago in the sand, we choose our steps in the present and can alter our path moving forward without being tethered to our past.

I often wish parts of my past could be washed away. Forgiveness has a similar effect. It is a merciful gift from God that we sometimes genuinely experience through the forgiveness of people we have hurt in some way. To borrow an important Buddhist concept, we should live as if life is impermanent, one step at a time and always ripe with opportunities for good choices. Nevertheless, all that we do and say, good and bad, leaves a mark like Luke's hand on the porch. This realization can be a powerful motivation for more focused day-to-day qualitative living.

There is a creative tension between seeking to live in the present moment, being responsible for our past actions, and moving ahead into the future. We do not want to live in our past, but we certainly want to learn from it. We also want to avoid becoming lost in dreams of the future, yet we should embrace the potential for newness and change as we look ahead. The point is we are accountable for what we have done and free to make better choices in the future. The important intersection is our present moment.

Jesus modeled living in the moment as he met and responded to needs everywhere he went. His teachings reflect the same emphasis. In the Sermon on the Mount, Jesus told his followers: "The eye is the lamp of the body. So, if your eye is healthy, your whole body will be full of light; but if your eye is unhealthy, your whole body will be full of darkness" (Mt 6:22–23). Our eye is our focus in life, which should be on the present moment, attune and open to opportunities for love, caring, and service. The past and future are important primarily as they inform and sharpen our attention to the present.

The apostle Paul placed a high value on conduct. Paul's New Testament letters also indicate that he believed in an imminent return of Jesus to the earth and an end to the present order. Thus, the present moment had heightened significance for Paul. In his letter to the Ephesians, he emphasized: "Be careful then how you live . . . making the most of the time" (Eph 5:15–16). Well, the world did not end, but Paul's injunction is timeless. How we live is critically important; therefore, we should be focused and judicious in each of our words and actions, letting our "gentleness be known to everyone" as Paul suggests in another epistle (Phil 4:5).

Back on my porch with the sun up, I think of my dad holding my hand long ago and am grateful for all who have helped and cared for me in days gone by. As thoughts turn again to grandchildren, I smile in anticipation of joyously watching them grow. Inspired and energized, I get up to live with my eye on this day.

Chapter 19

Before and After

"Are you OK?" I barely heard those words from my good friend and longtime running buddy, Dean, in the spring of 2011. We were on an early Thursday morning run from the Town Lake YMCA, starting one of a few loops we have run together for more than twenty years now. This day, however, was very different for me. We were barely a mile into the run, and I felt terrible. Dean heard me wheezing and sensed me really slowing down. I felt like I was running under water. I could not catch my breath. I stopped, asked him to go on, and sluggishly walked back to the Y by way of the closest bridge over the river.

Back at the club, I sat on a bench in the locker room with my head in my hands. The walk to my car in the parking lot felt like a marathon. I called my longtime doctor and friend and went straight to his office. After an EKG, he said he hoped I did not have plans that day, and if so, to cancel them. "You have AFib." I had never heard of it and always thought my heart was as healthy as it could be. "It is," he said, "but this is a rhythm issue and not a heart disease matter."

It was barely nine o'clock in the morning as I stubbornly walked across 38th Street to the Heart Hospital to meet my electrophysiologist (had never heard of that either) for the first time. His assistant greeted me and said I was "theirs" now. Runners will all understand the first question I asked my new doctor: "Can I still run?"

"Yes, and you should more now than ever, but things will be different."

That was a pivotal day. It is a point of reference as any "before" and "after" event in my life. I am most fortunate that this condition is somewhat manageable. Unfortunately for me, the smallest dose of medication turns me to a zombie with a heart rate into the thirties, but it is a condition subject to possible surgical correction. For now and possibly for the rest of my life, AFib negatively affects my desired activity level and absolutely wrecks some days when I am in the AFib zone with attendant side effects. It is a fairly common malady and pales in comparison to other diagnoses, but for me it is a big deal.

On that scary day years ago, I seriously contemplated my mortality as I walked from my GP's office to the Heart Hospital. I felt terrible and had no idea what was ahead. I called my wife in her second-grade classroom, our two children, and my brother in his office in Atlanta. I had difficulty speaking, but inside I was certainly focused on both the people I love most and my life journey. *How had I lived to that point? What should I change given the opportunity?* I wondered.

Contemplation of the end of our lives is encouraged in some religious traditions. In his book *The Lost Art of Compassion* (Harper Collins 2004), which integrates Buddhist concepts with aspects of American psychology, Lorne Ladner emphasizes the importance of such an exercise. The purpose of such meditative attention is not to be morbid; rather, it can awaken us to the importance of today and those around us. Regardless of people's position on an afterlife or not, we do not have forever in this world. Most of us do not yet want to leave it, but we all will. We should not be preoccupied with death, but truly and calmly facing its certainty can enable us to make the most of our time today.

Within our time on earth, we also experience moving through seasons of life, such as those related to aging, work, and family as well as health changes. The inquisitive author of the Book of Ecclesiastes, best thought of as simply the Teacher, captured this phenomenon in chapter three of his unique and surprisingly canonical work: "For everything there is a season, and a time for every matter under heaven" (Eccl 3:1). If you are close at all to my age (sixty-three), you can easily continue with "a time to be born, and a time to die," (v. 2) thanks to the Byrds capturing this eloquence in their 1965 rendition of Pete Seeger's song "Turn, Turn, Turn." As we move from one period of existence to another, pondering the end or "death" of one and the newness of the next can also be a helpful process. Similar to facing our mortality, it can enable us to focus attention on today and consider positive changes and adjustments in light of our past.

In his significant book, *When All You Have Ever Wanted Isn't Enough* (Fireside 1986), Kushner explores the Teacher's journey through life as documented in Ecclesiastes to search for answers and discover meaning. Kushner's analysis and insights challenge his readers to take a hard look at their own lives. The wisdom Kushner gathers and suggests from reflection on the Teacher's experience is that we should actualize one day's worth of meaning at a time, being fully aware of opportunities and loved ones.

I ended my dark day on a cold table in the hospital, waiting to be "rebooted" by having my heart shocked. My wife asked if they would yell "clear!" first. Then the technician said to wait. Suddenly, the monitor showed that my heart corrected itself back into normal rhythm. I got dressed and went home, shaken and exhausted but so very thankful. I vowed to be thankful and do my best to embrace each day of the rest of my life.

Chapter 20

Life's Paradox of Order and Chaos

Is religious experience a reflection of creative order out of chaos or an unpredictable mixture of order and chaos? To me, the creation stories in the first three chapters of the Bible imply that the answer is both. There can be a predictable, enhanced order to a faith journey akin to the rhythmic, progressive seven-day account in Genesis (1:1–2:3). That description of the dawning of our world included six creative steps or days, culminating with God's creation of humankind (1:26–27), followed by a sabbatical day of rest. In contrast, the well-known narrative of our beginnings involving Adam, Eve, and the Garden of Eden in Genesis 2–3 is turbulent. Similarly, religious experience is often chaotic, but the disorder sometimes leads to a more profound experience of God.

In his book *Falling Upward* (Jossey-Bass 2011), Father Richard Rohr explores the spirituality of what Carl Jung and others have described as the "two halves of life." Essentially, one is characterized by orderly systems and the other by deviations from the structure. In a religious context, Rohr explores learning moral rules and religious institutional order to establish authority and a person's identity (part one), followed by embarking on journeys away from one's comfort zone to discover authentic faith and perhaps actually experience God (part two). Yet the sequence is not a strict bifurcation of life. Ideally, a person goes through each stage and the two pieces end up complementing and informing each other. For example, butting up against authority and exploration away from one's religious "home" can sometimes provide a path back with appreciation for the true heart of home and not just its walls.

Among the contemporary problems Rohr laments are that some people never had a foundational moral and belief system established by parents or religious institutions. Meanwhile, other people who did, got stuck and never moved beyond merely following rules and/or parroting creeds. The Gospels give us strong indication that Jesus ran into the brick wall of the latter types in positions of power within his own Jewish tradition. Although this conflict with the immovable establishment in large part cost him his life, Jesus by deed and word showed a way beyond such stiff regularity toward an actual experience of and with God.

In our orthodoxy, we sometimes forget that Jesus was somewhat radical and chaotic in his religious practice. One telling example: Jesus's conflict with those who demanded that the rules be followed at all costs relating to strict observance of the Sabbath, including not working. According to the Gospel of Mark, Jesus was hawked by some prominent Pharisees early in his ministry to see if he would work by healing someone who was in need on the Sabbath. Jesus healed a man with a withered hand in a synagogue. His judgmental stalkers then "immediately conspired . . . how to destroy him" (Mk 3:6). Before healing the man, Jesus had asked his critics, "Is it lawful to do good or to do harm on the Sabbath, to save life or to kill?" (v. 4). Asked differently, "Which is more important, the spirit of religious rules or strict observance of the unwavering letter of such rules?" The Sabbath laws were meant to promote good and not obliterate it. As Rohr observes in *Falling Upward*, however, sometimes "religious people tend to confuse the means with the actual goal." The potential danger is making rules and institutional observance our gods as opposed to appreciating them as God-given techniques and pathways intended to point us toward what is truly important.

Jesus deviated from the constructs of the legalism of his day; instead he focused on and experienced the objective of loving and caring for others in need. Yet Jesus was himself a rabbi. Rohr observes that "Jesus the Jew criticizes his own religion the most, yet never leaves it."

A most striking example of Jesus elevating the core above the letter of the law is recorded in John 8. Religious leaders brought a woman caught in adultery to Jesus, indicated that the law of Moses demanded her to be stoned to death, and asked him what to do as a test. The disparaged woman was not unlike the tax collectors, prostitutes, and others Jesus befriended, much to the chagrin of the Pharisaic power structure. Jesus told the crowd that anyone without sin should be the first to throw a stone. After the crowd dispersed, Jesus told the woman he did not condemn her either, that she should go her way, and "from now on do not sin again" (v. 11). Love and mercy won out over fundamental application of rules but without minimizing the importance of appropriate moral conduct.

When we reach out without judgment to others in need, even and perhaps especially when they are outside of our peer group or religious practice setting, we might well experience what God has intended for us all along.

Chapter 21

Sanctity of Friendship

"I have more than five hundred friends," she so proudly announced.

As I pondered this ecstatic utterance from my younger and technically savvy acquaintance, I recalled the booming voice of my law school Practice Court professor long ago: "Imprecise!" At least in my archaic and social media limited frame of reference, "friend" is a term carefully and reverently reserved for a few very special people in one's life.

The Book of Proverbs indicates that a "friend loves at all times" (17:17). It adds, "Some friends play at friendship but a true friend sticks closer than one's nearest kin" (18:24). Hundreds of people might know your name and have access to pictures of you eating breakfast in a scenic place, but bona fide friendship is something rare. It is an art and a high calling. The mutuality of giving and receiving the love and care of real friendship is one of the richest potential blessings in life.

An old gospel song tells us, "What a friend we have in Jesus." The Gospels also seem to indicate that Jesus had just a few close and genuine friends during his life. To borrow a current term, Jesus certainly had a lot of followers and an even greater number of alleged followers. Like us, I imagine Jesus had circles of acquaintances extending out from and around him.

From the outside in, these groups may have included, for example, listeners in the crowds (i.e., the Sermon on the Mount in Matthew 5–7), people he dined with, those who traveled with him, disciples, and the twelve apostles (eleven plus Judas Iscariot, the bad apple). I suspect that in the closest circle around him, Jesus had a short list of very best friends.

We can be open, unguarded, and vulnerable within our inner circle of friends. We often share our highest and lowest points and count on their companionship. In Mark 9, Jesus took only Peter, James, and John up a high mountain where he was transfigured before them and stood "dazzling white" with Moses and Elijah as God said from a cloud that Jesus is his "beloved son" (Mk 9:2–7). In Mark 14, Jesus took these same three friends apart with him in the Garden of Gethsemane before his arrest and betrayal as he "began to be distressed and agitated" and was "deeply grieved, even to death" (14: 33–34). Although Peter, James, and John did not fully understand the mountaintop experience and had trouble staying awake in the dark garden, they were *with* Jesus in both places and an integral part of each experience.

The eleventh chapter of John includes the miracle of Jesus raising Lazarus from the dead. Another miracle permeates the entire account: friendship. Lazarus and his sisters, Mary and Martha, were obviously good friends with Jesus. Before Lazarus died, Jesus received a message from his sisters that "he whom you love is ill" (Jn 11:3). Lazarus was dead when Jesus arrived and came upon a scene of mourning and deep sorrow among Mary, Martha, and those who lived near them. John tells us that Jesus was "greatly disturbed in spirit and deeply moved" and that he "began to weep." Some of those nearby observed and said, "See how he loved him" (vv. 33–36).

Many of us have experienced the overwhelming heartbreak of losing a very close friend, as well as the added intensity when such friend is also a near kin. Unlike Jesus, we do not summon our friend out of the tomb. Like Jesus, however, we truly lament because we have lost someone special and irreplaceable. We are richly blessed when we have more than one intimate friend, but they are not interchangeable. Rather, each is a unique and essential part of our life. Something important is missing when they are gone.

At the end of his life, Jesus had very close friends near him at the foot of the cross, weeping for him as he had wept for Lazarus. Two of the brave group who dared get so close were his mother, Mary, and the "disciple whom he loved" (Jn 19:26), thought by some in the Christian tradition to be the apostle John. With a few of his very last words before death, Jesus expressed the absolute trust reserved for real friends when he said to Mary, "Woman, here is your son," and to John, "Here is your mother." His close friend John took it to heart because "from that hour the disciple took her into his own home" (vv. 26–27).

Friends should be treasured and embraced while they are with us, yet the gift and power of authentic friendship lasts forever.

CHAPTER 22

Living without Waiting

"I don't think Skippy shares our conception of his disease. I bet he feels today pretty much like he felt yesterday and the day before. He gets up, eats, plays, maybe chases a chipmunk or two. That's his day. He's living. He's not waiting."

Skippy the dog is one of many animals in Neil Abramson's *Unsaid* (Hachette 2011), a must read for any animal lover. Skippy has a heart condition that will soon take his life. The words above are of consolation from a wise and caring veterinarian to Skippy's caretaker and the mother of a special needs child who is quite attached to this canine friend.

One of the human characters in Abramson's book is David, a New York attorney who is grieving the premature death of his wife, Helena. The novel is written from Helena's perspective. At a point where David shows signs of healing and truly paying attention to the moment, Helena observes, "He's not between places or in resistance to where the day finds him." Like his best friend Skippy, David is actually alive.

One of my truly developed skills is one I would like to lose. I am a master at anticipating and planning, then often re-planning, the next phase of my life. Whether it is getting through adolescence or college or my first job or even today in anticipation of tomorrow, too much of life has been a preparation and bridge of sorts to the next step. I continue my journey to trade this inclination in for a mind-set and lifestyle that fully embrace and are attentive to the present moment and everyone and everything around me. Old habits die hard, but discipline in daily habits can aid in transformation.

In the New Testament, the apostle Paul encourages his first century readers to endeavor to be Christ-like. For example, he enjoins his friends at Philippi to lead lives "worthy of the gospel of Christ" (Phil 1:27). The decades old J. B. Phillips translation of this verse says, "[M]ake sure your everyday life is worthy of the gospel of Christ" (J. B. Phillips Version). Jesus is Paul's model and the model for all Christians. The Gospels give us a glimpse of the everyday life of Jesus. One key item for Jesus appears to be his daily practice of starting very early with a walk, prayer, and reflection. For example, early in his busy public ministry, Mark tells us that Jesus rose very early before daylight to go out to a "deserted place" to pray, such that his disciples had to hunt for him (Mk 1:35–36).

Every day of life can go by without a personal reminder to be awake in it and open to its opportunities, including ministering to others with needs and simply embracing the goodness of life. A quiet time alone, being still, and zooming in on the day at hand is an acquired skill that is developed with practice and repetition. Attending to each moment of life does not happen spontaneously or in direct response to one's realization of the value of being in focus. A day or a week or any other period of time should not be something to get through in order to move on to something else we deem more important or better in some way. No day is dispensable; rather, each day is life itself.

In the Sermon on the Mount in Matthew, Jesus taught his followers to have their eyes on the moment and not to be anxious about the future: "[D]o not worry about tomorrow, for tomorrow will bring worries of its own. Today's trouble is enough for today" (6:34). Jesus drew on images from nature in the preceding verses, including references to birds and flowers. We can learn a lot from God's creation and critters. My dog Copper, unlike Skippy in the novel *Unsaid*, is healthy and vibrant. Like Skippy and most any canine friend, however, Copper lives in the moment. Each of his days has a nice rhythm to it. I learn from him in many ways. When I focus on certain routines, like an intentional prayer, reflection, and quiet time each morning to remind me what is really important, I am less inclined to rush the day to get to the next and do a much better job of being thankful now.

At the end of my summer break from teaching, and before the start of a busy fall law school quarter a few years ago, my wife and I spent time with dear friends in Colorado to escape the heat. Each morning, I walked in what seemed like a paradise with my longtime close friend Jim and his faithful dog Scooter, who might well be the sweetest and most well-behaved dog on earth. At the end of our outing one morning, I stayed outside with Scooter on the small town's main street as Jim went into a bakery to get our breakfast. We were approached by a woman with a special needs son in his twenties. The young man's eyes lit up when he saw Scooter. He petted Scooter, and Scooter responded with his beautiful eyes, wet kiss, and wagging tail. He greets everyone this way, without distinction. As Mom and son walked off with big smiles, I stood there with a tear in my eye. God spoke to me in that quiet, clear mountain air through his dear creature, who was fully attune to the situation and reacted in a gentle, loving manner. I hope and pray I can take the lesson to heart every day for the rest of my life.

Chapter 23

Wake up and Give Thanks

It was one of those mornings. After a bad night's sleep and preoccupation with work-related minutiae during waking intervals, I slogged to the coffee pot and shuffled to my study. I sat down with my dog and too quickly went through the motions of my morning reading and quiet time. My mind, however, was light-years from my tranquil objective. My usual treasured morning time was more whining than spiritual meditation. Finally, I made it to the health club to meet my good friend for our weekly run and visit. My daily focus so far was sour, focused on every ache, pain, and problem I felt or could imagine.

Then it happened. The polite and always friendly young man at the counter encouraged me to "have a nice run" as I started to snarl out the door to the trail. He was thirty years or more my junior, but in that moment, he was my elder and teacher. A slap in the face or a water cooler full of icy Gatorade on my back could not have awakened me more to the day and its blessings and opportunities. Unlike me, my young friend had chosen the right attitude that morning. He spoke his kind words without a trace of bitterness or envy from his wheelchair. It immediately transformed me.

I just said, "Thank you," and headed out the door into what was all of a sudden, the cool and peaceful morning I had chosen to miss up to that point.

Have you ever turned your eyes around? I had that morning. They were turned inside so that all I could see was myself—as in my self-absorbed self! In contrast, my friend's eyes were wide open, turned out to look at and touch others. His model corrected my focus.

Reflecting without much conversation on my run that morning, I took ownership of the self-pity skewing my perspective on life earlier when I rolled out of bed.

Years before on a cold and rare icy morning in Austin, I had chiseled a thick layer of ice off of our steep driveway with an old-fashioned weed blade. It was ill-advised to say the least (not a high IQ moment for me). I was in my usual rush with a type-A determined frenzy to drive one hundred dangerous miles to teach my class, despite my wife's wise counsel that my students would welcome a walk. I furiously hacked away with discomfort until I felt a snap accompanied by acute pain high in my hamstring. I could barely walk, and each step hurt.

After decades of running every morning, it would be five months before I took my next compromised running steps. Yet I did take those steps and was able to progress from a strange leg injury. I continue to learn from the challenge and am thankful for the countless blessings I can enjoy through being active. Yet I can still descend into the negative, insular cycle of despair and regret about something I cannot undo, and which, in the greater scheme of things, is not that big a deal.

At the close of her meaningful book *Mile Markers* (Roadale 2011), Kristin Armstrong focuses on the importance of gratitude. She challenges readers to set gratitude as a "default" starting point and describes the significance of a "gratitude attitude." That simple phrase encapsulates the spirit of sincere thanksgiving as a chosen frame of mind and way of life that is at the heart of legitimate religious traditions.

In his letter to the Philippians, St. Paul enjoins his readers not to "worry about anything, but in everything by prayer and supplication with thanksgiving let your requests be made known to God." The result will be "the peace of God [beyond] all understanding" guarding one's heart and mind (4:6–7). In Psalm 34, the psalmist proclaims, "I sought the Lord, and he answered me, and delivered me from all my fears" (v. 4).

When I awake each day, I often find that if I calmly and honestly speak my troubles in the context of thankfulness, the result will be serenity, which I can experience throughout the day if I persevere with the right disposition. In contrast, if I start off on the wrong foot into a negative cycle, God often anticipates my prayers before I utter them and rescues me via friends picking me up and reminding me of the better path.

Returning from our run that morning, I walked back into the health club to even more pleasant words from my friend, "How was your run this beautiful morning?" Although I awoke a bitter person that day, I emerged most thankful for a true example of a grateful spirit. I resolved again to meet and work through my own challenges with a more consistent perspective of thanksgiving.

Chapter 24

Qualitative Living on the Narrow Path

Recently as I was preparing to teach a Water Law class, I felt overly stressed because we were behind my neatly planned syllabus and the quarter was nearing its end. I pondered how in the world we were going to cover all of the material I had planned in such a short amount of time. I never liked interminable evening makeup sessions as a way of catching up when I was in law school ages ago, so I refused to make that the answer. Then I heard the wise voice of a professorial mentor and good friend who suggested when I first started teaching, "*How* you cover material is more important than *how much* material you cover." Eureka! I needed that reminder. So, I transitioned and decided to start my class with a stated objective for the day's session: "Our goal today is to cover a lot of ground efficiently but without getting in a hurry." More importantly, I made a mental note for myself before class to take it slow and stay centered.

As important as that class is to me, I realized that my academic reawakening had even more significant applicability for retuning to my day-to-day life. Qualitative experience trumps quantitative activity. I need shorter to-do lists with a single-tasking perspective instead of a mega-tasking approach in my life. I want to pay more attention to people and things around me and pay less attention to checking off multiple bullet points marking completed tasks. The "how much can I get done?" mentality usually translates into an uncomfortable, frenzied mode that has me constantly looking ahead at the rest of my list. Transforming my daily approach to life, however, is much easier for a type-A person like me to articulate than to actualize.

Doing one thing at a time with intention and awareness is a challenging and high calling. In the Sermon on the Mount, Jesus says that "the gate is wide and the road is easy that leads to destruction [but] . . . the gate is narrow and the road is hard that leads to life, and there are few who find it" (Mt 7:13–14). It is difficult to stay on a thin line without complete focus on the present. Keying into an earlier part of this important collection of teachings in the Gospel of Matthew, one needs an "eye [that] is healthy" as a "lamp of the body" (6:22) to travel the narrow way.

My experience as a trail runner on a single channel trail as opposed to a wider course illuminates for me a dimension of the narrow path metaphor. A solitary track often has barely enough room to place one foot in front of the other while meandering over roots and rocks through a forest. Any lapse from full attention to each momentary step with eyes open, front and center, can mean falling off of the intended route or worse yet, a painful face-plant. For those (not me) brave enough to traverse the dark woods at night, an actual headlamp is needed to see. In contrast, a broad trail is much easier and affords several luxuries, such as looking around as well as behind and ahead instead of paying strict attention to the detail of one's next move.

Along the narrow way, the past is significant because it informs the present. Although the road uniquely unfolds each day, indeed every moment, good and bad steps we have taken before in the midst of obstacles enable us to better find our way now. The future, however, is but a dream until it materializes when each foot hits the ground.

People sometimes refer to what they might reflect upon while on their deathbed, such as wishing they had paid more attention to certain people (family and friends) and things they truly enjoyed in life (as opposed to extremes of time at the workplace). I hope to avoid any deathbed experience. I prefer to die instantaneously while being active. Ideally, doing something meaningful and enjoyable with someone I love would be especially nice. Nevertheless, the occasional mental exercise of imagining our life is over can help us focus on what we are doing today—and why, as well as potentially redirect us to what is truly sacred and worthwhile.

Chapter 25

True Wealth

"He has more money than God." I have heard this many times during my life as a description of some person with a whole lot of money and prestige. I know it is just a so-called expression. When I heard it recently, however, I shook my head a bit and realized just how ridiculous it sounded. It seems to me that everyone with a few cents has more money than God. It makes little sense to associate God with financial strength.

Money can be a hindrance to faith as well as an avenue of expression of faith. In the Christian tradition, the New Testament has a lot to say directly and indirectly about money. Jesus drew from a rich Jewish heritage full of concern for the poor, including the principle of thinking first of the needy with a charitable tithe of one's produce and a prophetic tradition denouncing worship practices unaccompanied by acts of mercy and justice.

Although Jesus has been and still is used to support alleged "gospels of wealth," it is obvious in reading the Gospels that Jesus was not a wealthy man. Rather, he usually associated with the poor and warned of the dangers of being rich. For example, in the Sermon on the Mount, Jesus said, "No one can serve two masters.. . . . You cannot serve God and wealth. Therefore I tell you, do not worry about your life" (Mt 6:24–25). Abundance can breed an insatiable appetite for more. It potentially adds stress and anxiety to one's life.

In a striking passage in Matthew 19, Jesus suggested to an inquiring rich young man that selling his possessions and giving to the poor might lead to perfection. When the man went away in grief, Jesus told his followers that "it is easier for a camel to go through the eye of a needle than for someone who is rich to enter the kingdom of God" (v. 24). Jesus taught with astounding images to get people's attention. The point is not that it is impossible for a rich person to live in God's kingdom. Rather, the kingdom experience, which includes serving and loving others and resting in God's peace, can be more difficult for a wealthy person.

The Epistle of James, probably better understood as the Wisdom of James, focuses significant attention on the rich. Prominently at the outset, the author instructs his readers, "Let the brother who is lowly boast in being raised up, and the rich in being brought low, because the rich will disappear like a flower in the field . . . in the midst of a busy life, [the rich] will wither away" (1:9–11). James also chastises those who constantly plan ahead in a moneymaking frame of mind:

> Come now, you who say, "Today or tomorrow we will go to such and such a town and spend a year there, doing business and making money." Yet you do not even know what tomorrow will bring. What is your life? For you are a mist that appears for a little while and then vanishes . . . you boast in your arrogance; all such boasting is evil. (4:13–16)

The *fact* of wealth is not the problem; rather, being wealthy presents significant faith *challenges* to stay humble, tune in to people around us, and focus on what should be real priorities in life. As the apostle Paul so aptly tells his protégé Timothy in a letter, "For the love of money is a root of all kinds of evil, and in their eagerness to be rich some have wandered away from the faith and pierced themselves with many pains" (1 Tm. 6:10).

It is noteworthy that even though Jesus associated to a great extent with the poor and needy and clashed with certain wealthy, prominent leaders of his day, Jesus also appears to have had some key friends of means. Nicodemus and Joseph of Arimathea are two prominent examples. John 3 records the account of Nicodemus, a Jewish leader, visiting Jesus to talk about God's kingdom and Spirit. Later in the Gospel of John after Jesus dies on the cross, Joseph, "who was a disciple of Jesus," removed the body of Jesus and Nicodemus assisted in providing a customary Jewish burial (Jn 19:38–40). Mark tells us that Joseph was a "respected member of the [Jewish] council" (Mk 15:43). Matthew adds that he was a "rich man" (Mt 27:57).

During his life and ministry, the Gospels tell us that many women not only followed Jesus but supported his travel and activities. At least one of these appears to have been well off by her description. According to Luke, Joanna, "the wife of Herod's steward Chuza," was among the "many . . . who provided for him out of their resources" (Lk 8:3).

Similar to these examples of faith during the life of Jesus and after his death, using our financial resources to quietly help others in need is a legitimate and important way to actualize our faith. Money can be a powerful tool of good when it is not hoarded as an end in itself.

Chapter 26

Embracing Fatigue and Opportunity

After an hour and a half on the trails in the heat and humidity of a long Texas summer, I was physically spent. I had started running at the first hint of daylight at St. Edward's Park, a delightful venue and one of my favorite trail access points in Austin. When I stopped, I experienced a drained sense of integrated calm and contentment.

Although it is not always welcome in our lives, fatigue can be a spiritual ally that helps to slow us down and become more centered. Perhaps the triggers of fatigue in part signal whether it is potentially friend or foe. In his classic book, *The Screwtape Letters* (Geoffrey Bles 1942), C. S. Lewis creatively deals with healthy and unhealthy aspects of the spiritual journey. At one point, he observes that fatigue can be productive and result in gentleness, calm, and vision of sorts. Alternatively, when unexpected demands mount up to induce fatigue and alter our planned lifestyles and hopes, the result can be anger and extreme frustration. Neither of these is conducive to spiritual well-being. Our response to such challenges, of course, is what truly augments such unhappiness.

The Gospels record miraculous stories from the life of Jesus. One prominent one is the feeding of five thousand people with very little food. A truly remarkable aspect of this event, which kind of sleeps beside the more prominent miracle, is the perseverance of the apostles through exhaustion to respond to changed circumstances by helping meet the needs of the crowd.

As Mark tells the story, it starts with this inner circle of followers gathering around Jesus after an active period of work and teaching to talk with Jesus about what they had done. Obviously, they were exhausted from good but very tiring work. Mark tells us that "[Jesus] said to them: 'Come away to a deserted place all by yourselves and rest a while.' For many were coming and going, and they had no leisure even to eat. And they went away in the boat to a deserted place by themselves" (Mk 6:31–32). That vivid picture of a comforting reward of down time alone sounds awesome. In the midst of their collective fatigue, however, unexpected opportunity arose. A crowd had followed them and to their surprise, awaited on the shore when their boat arrived.

The Gospel tells us that Jesus had compassion on the crowd and taught them many things into the late hours of the day. I feel pretty sure the apostles were gritting their teeth through these teachings, wishing they had displayed the "do not disturb" sail on the boat to ward off any intruders into their highly anticipated sanctuary of rest. At the end of the day, they asked Jesus to send the crowd away, so that each person could get their own supper elsewhere (and the apostles start their promised, coveted rest period). Jesus answered them with a challenge that seems to illuminate an opportunity in time more important than starting their sabbatical: "You give them something to eat" (v. 37). After a little grumbling, but with the help of divine touch, they did just that, such that all ate and were filled and there were leftovers for future needs.

This powerful account tells me that true rest following good, ordered work is a godly necessity. We should be attune to our individual health and well-being but always open to people and needs around us. When we are really tired and a pressing need arises, we might well need help, both God's help and assistance from others. Sometimes these are one and the same.

In addition to embracing opportunities to help others, we should embrace calm time alone on a regular basis to regenerate and refocus. Being tired out can work in our favor, and in some cases, inducing a level of fatigue can help us slow down enough to relax. Earlier in Mark, we see Jesus getting up before anyone else "while it was still very dark" to go way out "to a deserted place" to pray and be alone (1:35). Soon after, he was very busy going about and being pressed by multitudes in need. What an excellent model for us: the quiet before and after the storm, as well, to help us cope with the stormy portions of our lives.

Chapter 27

Making the Workplace a Sanctuary

My guess is that most working people think in terms of escaping *from* instead of *to* the office or other workplace. How transformational might it be if we could experience work as a sanctuary of sorts?

In his thought-provoking book *Being God's Partner* (Jewish Lights Publishing 1994), Rabbi Jeffrey Salkin encourages readers to practically apply faith in all aspects of life and especially in their daily work. Although Salkin's book addresses primarily a Jewish audience with some reference to Christian principles, it is full of suggestions to make the routine work anyone does each day more meaningful and fulfilling. Salkin's ideas are applicable to a wide variety of workplaces, including traditional jobs as well as full-time parenting or retirement lifestyles, in other words, whatever we routinely do with most of our time from day to day. The heart of Salkin's approach is that life is a whole and our faith is fully applicable to all of it. Neither work nor any other aspect of life should be carved out.

One of Salkin's most intriguing recommendations in *Being God's Partner* is to "transform the office into a sanctuary." At first blush, this is counterintuitive because "workplace" and "sanctuary" seem like antonyms. Like most things in life, however, the potential congruence of the two has a lot to do with our chosen attitude and response action to our work. We can often choose to redefine and, better yet, create something new in our work experiences.

Sanctuary is a multifaceted term and concept. For example, it means a sacred place where we can experience God. Many people immediately think of their Sabbath or day of worship when they are far away from work. Salkin encourages us, however, to actively live out the sacred every day by reflecting God's character in all that we do. He reminds his Jewish friends of what God said to Moses in the book of Leviticus: "You shall be holy, for I the Lord your God am holy" (19:2).

Although Leviticus is sometimes thought of as a priest's manual of sorts, the injunction to be holy is from the heart of the book known as the Holiness Code and is intended for "all the congregation of the people" (v. 2). Being holy is for every day and every place and involves what we do. For example, we should "not defraud [our] neighbor" or "render an unjust judgment" (vv. 13, 15). Rather, God told the people through Moses to "love your neighbor as yourself" (v. 18) and to extend the same to outsiders because the "alien who resides with you shall be to you as the citizen among you" (v. 34).

Holiness Code concepts are central to Christianity as well as Judaism. Christians are called to follow Jesus as the manifestation of God. As the author of Colossians succinctly reminds followers, "As God's chosen ones, holy and beloved, clothe yourselves with compassion, kindness, humility, [gentleness], and patience" (3:12). Compassion and humility are among the traits Salkin asks us to implement daily. Another is creativity. Just as God in the first chapter of Genesis created everything in a step-by-step fashion before acknowledging the goodness of creation (including humankind) and resting, so we should seek to be creative and develop a rhythmic order in our work with periodic rest.

In addition to a sacred place to experience God, sanctuary also means a place of safety. For many of us, the office or other work setting feels far from a safe haven. Linking this notion of sanctuary with seeking to be holy like God (by being compassionate and loving others), allows for a shift in focus, which might change things. What if instead of focusing on transforming our everyday locale into a personal sanctuary, we did all that we could to help others experience it? This means including coworkers, customers, friends, children and whomever we "work" with each day. If we strive to help them feel safe by prioritizing, encouraging, affirming, and treating them fairly, and we work to help them achieve excellence and creativity, then we might take a huge step toward experiencing a sanctuary of sorts ourselves.

Despite our best efforts with God's help to enhance the quality of our and our neighbors' work life, there are often failures, missed opportunities, unfulfilled goals, and other major disappointments. Another biblical model applies here: re-creation. Examples of biblical re-creation include: the story of Noah in Genesis, deliverance from Egypt and emergence from the wilderness, return from exile with a new covenant and a new heart, and the concepts of new life. All represent a rich Judeo-Christian heritage of new beginnings. Being a partner with God, we can endeavor to rebuild our sanctuaries and help others rebuild and maintain their own sanctuaries in, through, and beyond dark times.

Chapter 28

Neighboring without Delay

At the start of a new season, especially anticipating Christmas holidays and a new year, I sometimes experience a tension between the comfort of traditional routines and a yearning for a newness that I can truly feel daily. We could search far and wide for something spiritually novel, but would it not be easier just to look next door or across the street? How about in our own home as well?

December means Advent for many Christians. A common meaning of the word "advent" is the coming of a notable person. That means Jesus for Christians. Each year, we remember for a month of Sundays leading up to Christmas, through various kinds of reenactment, his birth into the world long ago.

Oftentimes, the emphasis during the Advent season is on slowing down and waiting in a prayerful and reflective way. I expect seasons leading up to special days and times in other faith traditions are similar. There are wonderful benefits to mindfully slowing down in an annual journey toward spiritual significance and renewal. Nevertheless, in an Advent season rich in hopeful anticipation, I am reminded that waiting is not always a good spiritual strategy. It depends on context. The "greatest commandments," as they are characterized in the Gospels, provide a good example. Drawing on his Jewish roots, Jesus tells us that it is most important to love God with all of your heart, soul, mind, and strength and to "love your neighbor as yourself" (Mk 12:29–31; Dt 6:5; Lv 19:18). Loving God and experiencing God's presence can involve prayerful expectation and stillness, but manifesting our love by actively and practically caring for others calls for action now.

In *The Art of Neighboring* (Baker Books 2012), Jay Pathak and Dave Runyon encourage us to meet and establish relationships with the people who reside closest to us in our actual neighborhoods. This is not always comfortable. Praying for the best methodology or just an opportunity to meet the guy next door, then waiting for an answer might cloak our apprehension and keep us from simply taking the initial step to say hello. The authors' encouragement to "just do something" is illuminating. Sometimes when we have choices of good alternatives, it is helpful to remember that *how* we live out whatever choice we make is most important.

My understanding is that many churches in Austin, Texas, and other communities have aptly embraced the excellent and practical ideas presented in *The Art of Neighboring.* What a beautiful idea, not only for Christians to take a key teaching of Jesus to heart and do something about it, but for other traditions as well. The core of authentic faith expression across genuine religious traditions is a life of action based on love and care for others. Practically being a good neighbor through acts of kindness day to day is a powerful way to implement and apply one's faith. Emphasizing the supreme importance of such a lifestyle can cut across and maybe even dissolve belief differences within and across faith traditions. It also works for people who want no part of any faith tradition but truly value peaceful, loving, and caring relationships as a route to being truly human.

The holiday season presents good opportunities for neighboring. "Open carry" of a plate of cookies or a loaf of fresh bread with a smile throughout one's neighborhood is good policy and practice. It can also start wonderful friendships close to home. What is more challenging for some this time of year, however, is dealing with strained family relationships. We might dread just being in the same room with a relative or two we only encounter once a year. Reaching out to a stranger across the street or next door might look pretty easy compared to forgiving a past wrong and starting anew in certain family relationships. Yet our families are our closest neighbors.

As we remember and await the presence of God or strive for a more meaningful life, whatever our tradition, it might be time to reach out in love without delay to a potential new friend close by, and perhaps more so, to a parent, child, or sibling.

Chapter 29

Living in the Light of Each Day

Wide-eyed and curious, I chased the chickens and other country critters before taking a big drink of ice-cold water pumped from a well. After drinking too much water, I visited for the first time in my life what my dad referred to as an "outhouse." As a young boy growing up in Tyler, I quickly realized that a trip to the farm in the fork in the road called Gresham was like stepping back in time. After the initial experience, we often returned for Sunday afternoon visits with Mom and Pop, my paternal great-grandparents. Other than the time my brother used a stick to lock me in the outhouse, I always had fun.

Not many years later and at the end of his long life, Pop passed away. Another first for me was going to his old-style funeral. That left more of a lasting impression than the old home. Although cognitively I realized people died, I was now truly acquainted with it. Beyond afraid, the fear sunk into my bones over the next several weeks. It also crept into my dreams whenever I had the good fortune to fall asleep, usually with the door open and a light on.

Now, decades later, when I let myself, I can still conjure up vivid images of Pop's body dressed in his only suit in the open casket. I see my strong grandfather nearby as I had never seen him, audibly sobbing with his head in his hands during the service. Outside of himself and not sure how he could help, I am unsure if my dad had ever seen his father so uncontrollably sad. I feared it all. It was a long time before I stopped imagining being in the casket myself and no longer alive as a human being. The deep darkness of the absence of life overwhelmed me.

How do we start to make peace with our mortality? How can we live with the certainty that life as we know it will inevitably end without letting that fact overshadow our days with fear of most everything? The extremes of avoidance of the subject and morbid daily preoccupation are bad strategies. Confidently talking about death being irrelevant because of expected eternal life in heaven can be a form of avoidance. Although I personally believe in a life beyond, that is different from facing the reality that our profoundly good gift of life from God will end with a return to dust.

In his essay "Death" in *Love and Living* (McGraw Hill 1979), the introspective and thought-provoking Merton suggests that death "contributes something decisive to the meaning of life." Strikingly, the book is a posthumous collection of Merton's writings. For Merton, death is simply the end of life and as such, part of its continuity. If we obsess over death, then we "give death a kind of power over life." It then operates "in the midst of life" instead of its end and strangles us with fear and unhealthy apprehension.

Rather than dominating our lives and thoughts, when we accept that life ends, it should *qualitatively inform* our living. Returning to my childhood, I recall another image from something else very new at my maternal grandmother's house—a color television. My grandmother watched a popular soap opera that opened with a jingle declaring our days to be "like sands through an hourglass." I visited her often and tried very hard to get that song out of my young head! Now I wonder about the image. If we compare the sum of our days to an hourglass, is life more akin to the passing of the sand from the top or the accumulation of sand in the bottom? In Ps 90:12, the psalmist prays, "[T]each us to count our days that we may gain a wise heart." Embracing life, we should intentionally live each day as a gift, "counting" each one as another opportunity to live, love, and serve. Instead of fretfully sensing them slipping away, we can perceive our days qualitatively, adding to a treasure chest of experiences.

For Christians each spring, Easter season in part is a spiritual focus on the meaningfulness of the life and death of Jesus and the springing forth of new life. For all of us in any faith tradition, consenting to the reality of our own lives having an end one day should transform our present into something new with fresh light. Far from a morbid subject, with a healthy and joyously counterintuitive perspective, knowing we will ultimately leave this world can accentuate our lives this very day.

Chapter 30

When Lightning Strikes

About a year ago, after several years of continuous teaching and practicing law, I was ready for a break. I had my sabbatical all planned out. I craved a relaxed, comfortably structured summer. Among other things, I would spend my time preparing a new Water Law course, running and hiking trails across central Texas, and resting.

At the threshold of it all when I finished grading spring final exams, I experienced that rare contentment with the full three-month expanse of time before me. I was home on a Friday night with my dog in my lap and a novel in my hands instead of a casebook or pile of opinions in front of me to read. I was chilled out as light rain hit the roof, expecting my wife home soon from a dinner with her friends.

Suddenly, what I thought of as "my summer" with everything I was anticipating abruptly changed. The rain intensified and my dog awoke and shook as it thundered mightily. We heard what sounded like a shotgun go off on top of us. I saw a white-hot flash of light through the window before everything in the house went dark. *That lightning was really close,* I thought. Within three minutes, there was a haze in the house and a burning smell. Several hours later, after the fire department had left, we tried to sleep with the assurance that the apparent small electrical fire was actually out. I also kept thinking about my brilliant decision a month earlier to increase my homeowner's insurance deductible five-fold in order to save a few hundred dollars of annual premium.

Oh well, I could still hit the trails and work off the negative energy. A few days later, however, an unexpected pain led to a doctor visit and the need for fairly immediate day surgery. That knocked out a chunk of my hoped-for primary summer exercise activity.

In the midst of what felt like an unfair darkness of sorts, I received a letter from a pen pal. For years, she has courageously faced a multitude of challenging health problems in a system that is far from attentive and responsive. She is in prison for the rest of her life because of bad choices and company earlier in life. Despite her circumstances, my friend encourages me and craves detailed news about our grandkids. In part she wrote, "I miss kids running around and playing. I haven't seen a child play in twenty years. Gosh, that's a long time."

With more of a wake-up call than lightning striking the house, I realized yet again in my life that I needed a perspective and attitude adjustment. It was time to exchange the mirror I often walk around with for a window. Even during wholesome seasons of rest and desired solitude, our eyes should be fully open and sensitive. Instead of focusing mostly on myself, I wanted to see and wake up to the people and life all around me. I needed to count and embrace my numerous blessings and reach out to help others, especially those with few if any bright spots in life. It was time for me to "wise up."

Wisdom in a religious sense is not about having a natural-born high IQ. Rather, the way of wisdom is open to everyone. Enlightenment results from learning and practical application.

Sources of wisdom are time-honored teachers and mentors along with life experiences. We are to consider, contemplate, and gather these treasures to enhance ourselves and the lives of people around us.

Within a traditional book of Judeo-Christian wisdom, a parent or teacher in Proverbs 4 encourages his children to pay attention and "gain insight" (Prv 4:1). This is a process that lasts a lifetime. We need to make good choices for our observation, focus, and learning. Good teachers and all of life's experiences should top the list toward progress for greater wisdom in our journey. The writer of Proverbs 4 also tells us that "the path of the righteous is like the light of dawn, which shines brighter and brighter until full day" (v. 18).

I hope lightning never hits the same place twice. When it comes to the path of life, however, I welcome striking illumination such as the letter from my friend to help refocus my attention on people and experiences all around me.

CHAPTER 31

Mental Nutrition

"If you can worry, you can meditate." As a lifelong world class worrier, John Ortberg's words in *If You Want to Walk on Water, You've Got to Get out of the Boat* (Zondervan 2001) grabbed my attention. In his practical style, Ortberg states simply, "To meditate merely means to think about something over and over."

Have you ever characterized yourself or someone else as a worrier? I have often thought of myself this way, as if it were an innate condition or personality type that I could not help. Laying aside the important nuances and depths of truly meditative disciplines and psychotherapy, in many cases (mine included), worry is a learned habit. We can create an apprehensive and fearful sense with years of practice. Over time, anxiety becomes ingrained.

In his letter to the Philippians, the apostle Paul encourages his readers to "think about" certain things, then act, resulting in the "God of peace [being] with you" (Phil 4:8–9). Paul's suggestions include "whatever is true, whatever is honorable, whatever is just, whatever is pure, whatever is pleasing, [and] whatever is commendable" (v. 8). At the end of this list, Paul says that "if there is anything worthy of praise, think about these things" (v. 8).

Turning good thinking into a fresh habit that edges a predominant mind-set of worry aside requires hard work and consistency. Ortberg suggests letting a good thought "simmer in your mind," then "reflecting on it from different angles *until it becomes part of you*" (emphasis added).

Improved thinking is one step. Acting on it makes us whole. In Paul's letter to the Colossians, he says to "*clothe yourselves* with compassion, kindness, humility, [gentleness], and patience. . . . Above all, clothe yourselves with love, which binds everything together in perfect harmony" (3:12, 14, emphasis added). We need to truly wear compassion around all day long. Although positive mental focus is important, merely keeping noble thoughts inside is empty.

Have you ever told someone facing difficulty that they are in your thoughts and prayers? I have said this to many people and heard it from others during personal challenges. These are often significant words of comfort in and of themselves. Prayerfully thinking of someone can be powerful. Sometimes, but not often enough, I slow down and listen to my prayers for someone in need. I then ask myself, "What can I *do* about the circumstances that might help?" In some cases, simple things like a phone call, handwritten note, or personal visit are comforting. Other times, providing a ride or a meal or sitting with a friend in a hospital is most helpful to the person in need as well as the provider.

The New Testament book of James succinctly links and also contrasts word and thought with deed. In a nutshell: "If any think they are religious" but never do anything about it, "their religion is worthless" (Jas 1:26). The author's examples of "pure and undefiled" religion include caring "for orphans and widows" (v. 27). In a striking example of alleged faith being dead without practical works, the author of James asks, "If a brother or sister is naked and lacks daily food, and one of you says to them, 'Go in peace; keep warm and eat your fill,' and yet you do not supply their bodily needs, what is the good of that?" (2:15–16)

The things I tend to fret about mostly relate to me. Working toward a routine of healthy mental clarity steeped in love can dissolve the worry. Translating such thought into daily acts of kindness results in a more meaningful existence. Suddenly, the things I used to stew over pale in importance.

CHAPTER 32

Social Justice Is Always in Season

Exercising social justice simply means actively loving others who are vulnerable and in need. More particularly, social justice includes fair treatment and provision of opportunities for everyone in a society, with special emphasis and concern for the poor and other disadvantaged people. This crucial emphasis on caring for others is always in order, but some cultural circumstances cry out for prioritizing equity.

Social justice is embedded in the fabric of Judeo-Christian tradition, reaching a high point of expression in certain prophets such as Amos. Although often popularly understood as predicting the future, biblical prophets primarily spoke to their own generation and its historical circumstances. Another word for prophet is "seer," as in clarity of vision and speech from God for their own times. When similar contexts arise in later times, however, a prophet's insightful words have renewed relevance and heightened importance.

What about Amos? His was the era of a divided kingdom of Israel with two separate countries: Israel, the Northern Kingdom and Judah, the Southern Kingdom. He spoke to Israel in the first half of the eighth century BC during a time of military strength and national security, a strong economy and extravagant wealth (for some) and thriving worship centers and related rituals. Many perceived these as signs of God's national favor, but Amos saw things differently.

Amos denounced the rich "who oppress the poor, who crush the needy" (Am 4:1). He pronounced judgment because they "trample on the poor . . . afflict the righteous . . . and push aside the needy in the gate" (5:11–12). Speaking for God at the summit of his message, Amos strongly declared to that self-assured generation: "I hate, I despise your festivals, and I take no delight in your solemn assemblies. . . . I will not accept [your religious offerings]. . . . Take away from me the noise of your songs. . . . But let justice roll down like waters, and righteousness like an ever-flowing stream" (vv. 21–24). This passage has sometimes been called the MLK passage because Martin Luther King Jr. applied it to violent racial discrimination in his time, the 1960s.

It is noteworthy that Amos himself was an apparent victim of social injustice. He was a foreigner from a small village, traveling north from his native Judah to Israel to proclaim God's word (1:1). Further, Amos was a shepherd and dresser of trees (1:1; 7:14), with a socioeconomic gulf between him and powerful political and religious leaders of Israel. In a moving autobiographical passage, Amaziah, the priest of the religious center in Bethel, accused Amos of conspiring against the king of Israel with his prophecy. Amaziah told Amos to go home and "never again prophesy at Bethel, for it is the king's sanctuary, and it is a temple of the kingdom" (7:10–13).

The appearance of holiness at a busy religious institution and assembly like Bethel did not make it or its people so. Amos's perspective was profound but not novel. Social justice runs deep in Jewish tradition. For example, God's words to Moses many generations earlier included a prominent Holiness Code that spoke of authentic holiness (Leviticus 19). "You shall love your neighbor as yourself" is part of this code (Lv 19:18). Jesus emphasized such love as one of the greatest commandments (Mk 12:31). But it is not just neighbors: "When an alien resides with you in your land, you shall not oppress the alien. The alien who resides with you shall be to you as the citizen among you; you shall love the alien as yourself" (Lv 19:33–34). Amos was oppressed as an alien. He was also from a different country and culture and had a different point of view from prominent leaders. As God's special messenger, Amos also championed the poor, needy, and others who were being oppressed in the land that he visited.

So, how do our times line up with early eighth century Israel? God always cares about living expressions of social justice—the rivers of true justice and righteousness take the form of loving, caring, and inclusive actions and initiatives. In the context of extreme wealth, military prowess, secure borders, and the illusion of religious prominence, Amos reminds us what God cares about and what is really important.

Chapter 33

United through Service

"Agreed to Differ, Resolved to Love, United to Serve." This profound Church Women United ("CWU") motto is the recipe for authentic intra-faith and interfaith relationships toward a common ground of doing good together. It could also work as an effective mission statement in families, organizations, and politics.

A few months ago on a nice Friday morning, I walked up the steps to the pulpit at Hyde Park Christian Church just a few blocks from where I lived when I was a University of Texas student in the mid-1970s. I occasionally have the privilege of speaking from a pulpit, but this was different. As I looked out at the almost full house of women only, I noticed that about half of the smiling, friendly, and supportive faces were black, and the other half were white. This good crowd was gathered to celebrate World Community Day. They were kind to invite me to share comments about the importance of social justice as part of their program.

Although I was there to speak, I was the one learning from their model. World Community Day was new to me along with the group that asked me to speak: CWU. World Community Day originated in the early 1940s during World War II with an emphasis on peace. Subsequently, certain Christian denominations set aside their theological and other differences to observe this day of unity through prayer and study. By the time of our celebration in November, and as the name "World Community Day" implies, the ecumenical, interfaith focus was broader. Common objectives included pursuing and actively practicing peace, compassion, respect, and understanding. Readings of similar expressions of the Golden Rule from major world religions highlighted the day's inclusiveness. Further, a bountiful collection of warm blankets for people in need on cold nights powerfully manifested interfaith bonding for cooperative service on this important day.

Similar to World Community Day, CWU began in the 1940s. The Austin Council of CWU began in 1940 to join Protestant, Catholic, and Orthodox Christian women together. Racially, theologically, and culturally diverse, these fine women unite to work for justice and peace. More particularly, in the 1940s, the intention was to bring white and black women together on an equal footing in a worshipful atmosphere. Under the same roof, they focused as one on what is truly important: the commonality of compassionate faith in action to help others in need and promote peace.

A CWU principle starts with a foundation for the whole: "Agreed to Differ." People and groups within and across religious denominational and faith boundaries must expect and respect differences in beliefs and traditions. When they do, they can then prioritize love and effectively work together. Religious tolerance does not mean giving up or compromising our own beliefs and practices. Rather, it sets us free to let go of judgment and dogmatic insistence that we have the doctrinal answers for everyone. Respectful tolerance opens us to the next principle: "Resolved to Love." After all, if there is one authentic faith-related "way" for everyone, it is the path of love.

Once we agree to differ and resolve to love, we can take the next step: "United to Serve." Do you ever shake your head at how much time and effort religious groups waste in guarded efforts to convince others that they are theologically "correct" in belief while others are "wrong"? Imagine what actual good could be done if the collective energy of all legitimate religious people worked instead toward helping others in poverty, sickness, and other needful circumstances.

In the Gospel of Luke from my tradition, John the Baptist received "the word of God . . . in the wilderness," then proclaimed a "baptism of repentance" (3:2–3). John told the "crowds that came out to be baptized" to "[b]ear fruits worthy of repentance" and not to rely on status as descendants of Abraham (vv. 7–8). Repentance is marked by a changed life, so "the crowds asked him, 'What then should we do?'" (v. 10). John's response gives us powerful examples of what a changed life looks like from a practical point of view: "Whoever has two coats must share with anyone who has none; and whoever has food must do likewise" (v. 11).

John's clarity that repentance actualizes in day-to-day acts of kindness and care of others is as authentic now as it was in John's time. With faith in action as our focus, we find common ground to bridge gaps within and outside of our own religious traditions and work together in a bond of love.

CHAPTER 34

Empathy and Compassionate Response

My dad loved dogs and hated squirrels. "Hate" is a word my parents avoided. Any time I ever used it as a young boy, such as related to onions or too much homework, my mother would say, "Honey, let's say it is not our favorite." Squirrels were not my father's favorite.

This past Father's Day, I had a unique reminder of my dad. I was attending our small group discussion at church. We focused on issues related to the afterlife (or not), including its relative importance in our faith and different images of it. We also emphasized one practical concept of immortality that I think most people can agree upon: the imprint and legacy we all leave behind by the way we lived. I certainly had my dad in mind, both the narrow moral path he showed me and thinking of him now in a blissful squirrel-free zone in heaven.

I arrived back home from church and hurried to the back door. I was anticipating the usual excited and warm greeting that awaited me from our sweet, normally passive rescue dachshund, Red. Whether I am gone for ten minutes or most of the day, Red typically greets me as if I just returned from a long voyage across the big pond. Surprisingly, Red was not at the door, wagging his tail with abandon. Instead, I discovered him in a corner of the yard in a stupor of sorts, panting, with a wild look in his eyes and limping. Then I saw his offering by the back door—it appeared to be a mortally wounded squirrel. I figured this to be the same squirrel who tormented Red daily by running along the fence line. Fortunately, Red avoided serious harm from his encounter with the squirrel and was back to himself by evening, sleeping on top of several towels on our couch.

After our church discussion and Red's surprise, I was even more focused on my dad. I recalled the time he struck a squirrel in the head with the sweet spot of a golf club after warning it, but only once, not to eat the crackers in his golf cart. My father was not perfect. That is part of what he taught me. Perfection can be a worthy faith-related moral objective, but we all have flaws to work through. In my tradition, Jesus taught us to aspire to perfection in his ethically rich and love-based Sermon on the Mount in Matthew 5–7: "Be perfect . . . as your heavenly Father is perfect" (5:48).

I was fortunate and blessed to have a father (and mother, brother, and other family mentors) who taught me so much by the way he lived. Dad was tolerant, inclusive, and consistent in how he treated people in his life with concern and care. True, he had his moments and would not have tolerated, for example, any suggestion of considering squirrels as sentient beings. Nevertheless, he consistently went out of his way to understand and help other people regardless of their differences or economic or other status.

Although my father seldom talked about any science of living, I vividly recall one occasion when he intentionally taught me the meaning and importance of empathy. I was maybe ten years old and had never heard such a big word. Empathy is all about identifying and sympathizing with others—one at a time—as a predicate to how we treat and respond to them. As my dad said those many years ago, "Son, put yourself in the other person's shoes in trying to understand and help that individual." While nuances of this fancy new word eluded me, I observed the concept in action. I immediately thought then and think back now to my dad calling workers by name and taking the opportunity to check on them most every time we went into the grocery store. Each week before daylight, on our trash pickup day, he would put out bottles of cold water for the tireless garbage collectors. These are a few examples of his countless practical acts of daily kindness. Over time, my dad turned this way of life into a habit. I saw clearly that empathy results in actual compassion.

Simplicity and a childlike perspective are good things, especially when we have or can find good behavioral models. I think the results have a lot to do with perfection in an authentic religious sense, cutting across different traditions with a unifying force. The Golden Rule is expressed in different formulations in major religious traditions, such as, "Do unto others as you would have them do unto you" (Christianity), and "What is hateful to you, do not do to your neighbor" (Judaism). Prioritizing empathy and compassionate response, daily in this and all of life, is our common vocation. It is the way God blesses us and how we bless one another, whatever our religious stripe.

Chapter 35

What Is "Justice"?

"Justice" is a word that people throw around in various contexts and with different modifiers, including "social justice." At its core, social justice means fair treatment, respect, and provision of opportunities for all people, with special concern for the poor and others who are disadvantaged compared to more fortunate persons. In our time of political extremism and a charged kind of nationalism pushed in sound bites, prioritizing social justice is controversial. Opponents might demonize it as the equivalent of social welfare or a hint of socialism with the prospect of higher taxes, while supporters might consider social justice initiatives at the heart of being authentically American. Politics and country aside, where does justice fit in a faith perspective and a faith-based life?

I heard a smug and demeaning comment once that social justice is never even mentioned in the Bible. I winced at this narrow, inerrant approach to Scripture, which lends itself so easily to supporting most any opinion. I prefer a more vibrant interpretive approach to the Bible, considering the nature and context of each part and prioritizing core emphases and common themes in the whole, such as love and nonviolence. After a few deep and mindful breaths, I asked about the strong emphasis on justice throughout Judeo-Christian Scripture. We might call this "biblical justice" or simply "justice" as it is characterized numerous times in the Bible.

Exercising justice is deeply rooted in religious traditions, including Judeo-Christian heritage, which is my personal focus. As a Christian, I consider Jesus the embodiment of justice. It is the heart of his life model and teaching as a rabbi and deeply sourced in his Jewish tradition. One high expression comes from the outset of the longest collection of Jesus's teachings in the New Testament, the Sermon on the Mount in Matthew 5–7. He starts by pronouncing the poor, the meek, and the targets of persecution as blessed and owning the kingdom of heaven (5:3, 5, 10). Elsewhere, when his adult followers tried to stifle and keep "little children" away with harsh words, Jesus instead welcomed them, saying "the kingdom of God belongs" to them (Mk 10:13–14). Jesus sought out, focused upon, and actively helped the poor, meek, persecuted, and children as well as the sick and others in need—all the intended recipients of what we term "social justice."

Jesus drew on his contemporary scriptures and tradition, which are still large parts of what Jewish (Hebrew Bible) and Christian (Old Testament) practitioners have in common today. The parable of the rich man and Lazarus (Lk 16:19–31) is demonstrative. As I recently heard a child describe it in a Bible school program, a parable is a small story with a huge message. Poor Lazarus laid starving at the gate of a wealthy man's property, but the rich man did not share anything with him, or even notice Lazarus. After they both died, the tormented rich man in Hades asked Abraham (with Lazarus beside him) across a chasm in the kingdom to warn his brothers to help the needy. Abraham responded that Moses and the prophets (what Jews and Christians have had in common now for about two thousand years) were all they needed to understand God's clear priority to exercise justice.

Numerous examples from the books of Moses (first five books of the Bible) and the Prophets cut across expanses of time and literary forms. A few representative examples include the story of Cain and Abel (Gn 4:1–16) and part of the Holiness Code (Leviticus 19) from the books of Moses, as well Isaiah and Micah, both prophets.

The Cain and Abel account is one of the ancient, etiological stories (of beginnings) in the first eleven chapters of the first book of the Bible and represents some of the oldest of all biblical sources. One brother was a farmer and the other a seminomadic shepherd. Cain killed Abel after thinking God accepted Abel's offering and rejected his. Tellingly, Cain asked God whether he was his "brother's keeper" (Gn 4:9). Cain is then banished as a fugitive. In part, the story condemns tribal hatred toward other groups of people and affirms the importance of all lives with the attendant responsibility to care for others by exercising justice.

The moral heart (Leviticus 19) of what is known as the Holiness Code (chapters 17–26) from the books of Moses is later in origin than the early part of Genesis. The ethical mandate is "[people] shall be holy" to reflect what God is like (19:2). Practically, this includes providing food for "the poor and the alien" (v. 10), paying laborers fairly (v. 13), and not harming the deaf or blind (v. 14). Prominently, it includes actively loving one's "neighbor" (v. 18) and "the alien as yourself" (v. 34), thus, exercising justice.

Much later than Mosaic laws, several prophets announced to their generations that God cares more about justice than anything, including worship. For example, God through Isaiah asks the "elders and princes" of his time, "What do you mean by crushing my people, by grinding the face of the poor?" (Is

3:14–15). Further, Micah highlights what is more important than religious worship or ritual. What God "require[s]" of his people is "to do justice, and to love kindness, and to walk humbly" (Mi 6:8).

Whether we call it social justice or anything else or just keep our mouths shut, truly caring for people should always be a contemporary and apolitical priority for all faith-based people. It is one religious issue where there should be no sides.

Chapter 36

What Are We Willing to See?

Years ago during a vacation in Colorado, I walked out of a bakery with a friend and his faithful dog, Scooter. I first introduced Scooter and Paul earlier in the chapter, "Living without Waiting." Scooter did not care that my friend and I wanted to rush home with the best sweet rolls ever so that we could get on with our meticulously planned day. He saw the reaction the young man with special needs, Paul, had to his presence. Paul lit up with a smile as he started petting his tail wagging new friend.

We introduced ourselves to Paul and visited with him and his mother. We lost track of time and our agenda for the day. We mostly answered Paul's canine-related questions to his mounting delight (the dog was now in his lap). Taking our cue from the observant never-in-a-hurry dog, we slowed down even more in the moment and shared our bounty of bakery treats. After saying our goodbyes, his mom thanked us with tears in her eyes. The thanksgiving ran both ways. I vividly recall Paul's smile and joy to this day along with the lesson I learned to be more aware of things and people around me each moment.

One of my favorite teachings of Jesus in the Gospel of Matthew emphasizes for me the importance of a fully aware and mindful focus. "The eye is the lamp of the body. So, if your eye is healthy, your whole body will be full of light" (6:22). Following shortly thereafter in this same collection of Jesus's teachings in Matthew, he says, "In everything do to others as you would have them do to you; for this is the law and the prophets" (7:12). The "law and the prophets" emphasize a strong Jewish foundation of this Golden Rule for Jesus and his contemporary followers. Although opening one's eyes to recognize needs, then working to meet them is easy to comprehend as a teaching, it is a challenging lifestyle. As Jesus said after reciting the Golden Rule, "[T]he gate is narrow and the road is hard that leads to life, and there are few who find it" (v. 14).

In contrast to this ethically and faith-based authentic way of life, it is easy to live with our eyes closed, which leads to misunderstanding. Growing up in the 1960s as a Beatles's music fan, I have heard and sung their version of this proverbial gospel-like saying countless times in the car or shower (mercifully for others, not publicly). The source is "Strawberry Fields Forever," released in the States as a single with "Penny Lane" on the (B) flip side. (For younger generations, this means an actual vinyl record for purchase at a local store to enjoy at home with a record player before the advent of cassette tapes, CDs, and online digital options.)

It is my understanding that Strawberry Field was an orphanage in Liverpool, England, near John Lennon's home. As a child, Lennon played with friends in a garden near the facility. I have no idea of any intended link between the closed eyes line and the orphanage when Lennon wrote the song. Nevertheless, the forever image of whether people recognize, then truly focus on helping orphans and others in obvious need is striking.

What do we choose to "see" or not see each day? My mind is too often lost and distracted from present surroundings via preoccupation with the past, future, or anything other than now. Thus, I miss opportunities to help others and enrich my own experience. Paying attention to others with clarity is the first step toward active charity, a priority shared by all legitimate faith traditions. I think that is what Jesus meant in his teaching and life-model. He asked his followers to look and recognize need (a healthy eye), then respond by actually helping others (using our healthy body now full of light).

In 1967, the Beatles also released one of their best and most creative albums, *Sgt. Pepper's Lonely Hearts Club Band.* One of the tracks, "Fixing a Hole," describes restoring the pleasure of a wandering mind by closing a hole where rain gets in. Personally, my overactive mind easily thinks in a multifaceted range far removed from today. Rather than habitually dispersed thoughts, I prefer to "fix" my mind in a different way, aspiring toward a sharp moment by moment focus. More particularly, I want my mind centered on others with full awareness of potential needs and opportunities around me right now and followed by appropriate response action. This essential shift in perspective involves full attention and discipline, but it is never too late to start or resume the hard work toward a narrow and meaningful path of life. I agree with the sentiment in the song about focusing on what is important now that was not considered important before.

CHAPTER 37

Life Experience and Faith

In the chapter "Living in the Light of Each Day," I shared my experience of attending my great-grandfather's funeral—my first funeral and my earliest truly sad memory.

I vividly recall walking by the casket with my dad and grandfather, Pop's son. I loved all three of these men dearly in respective degrees from my dad down to Pop.

Dad knew the funeral day would be hard on us. I suspect he spent a lot of time talking with my mother about whether my older brother and I should even attend but finally determined we should. Dad in particular did his best to prepare me for this first-time experience. I expect he knew looking at Pop's body would be tough on me and would also leave quite an impression. He was correct.

My dad emphasized to me several times before we left for the funeral home that it would not be Pop in the box. I walked by the casket in a line, beside my dad and grandfather. When I was just a few feet from Pop's body, I looked in. Other than the suit of clothes and tie, which I had never seen Pop wear, it sure looked like a pale and motionless Pop to me with closed eyes and a look on his face I had never seen or imagined.

The entire experience truly scared me. I had a hard time getting it out of my mind each day for a long time. It kept me awake at night for a while. I was frightened for Pop and afraid of what the future held one day for me. I kept thinking about being in a casket one day and tried hard to shake the claustrophobic image. I thought about Pop being underground in the casket. I strained to reassure myself that Pop was in heaven and his body simply returned to dust. I believed it then and still do, but on this side of the bridge—opposite of life in heaven—I was terrified.

I was not only impacted by Pop in death but the effect it had on the living. The hardest aspects of this memory are the sight and especially the sound of my grandfather. I loved him and saw him often. He was an integral part of my life. My granddaddy was a real character. He was a mountain of a man full of gentleness and generosity. He was fun to be around, and I treasured my time with him and my grandmother. On that day at the funeral service, however, sorrow overwhelmed him. He did not hold back his tears. When I get real still and think back on the experience, I can still hear him crying loudly. I had never seen him cry at all. It still breaks my heart to think about it and vividly remember. I also clearly recall the suffering look on my dad's face, mostly out of concern for his father. I expect he had never seen his dad in this extent of sadness and grief.

Whatever our religious affiliation, including mine as a Christian, life experiences significantly impact our faith journeys and perspectives. Scripture, worship, contemplative inquiry, teachings, prayer, and other aspects of our religion are certainly formative. Hopefully, they are also progressively influential in deepening and sharpening our beliefs and, more importantly, encouraging us toward ethical ways of daily living. Raw life experiences, good and bad, also define and impact our religious viewpoints. Some of them stay with us for a lifetime.

My first funeral experience and its aftermath impressed on me the realities of mortality, sorrow, grief, and fear. Through my parents and others who cared for me, I watched and learned how important our response actions are to negative life experiences, including our own and those of others. They wrapped their arms around me and one another. They encouraged me to talk about my feelings and fears and to remember Pop's legacy as a compassionate and fine man, another important aspect of immortality. This helped me understand how God is always with us, including hurting when we hurt. I experienced God in action and as a companion in the authentic, patient comfort and understanding from others. My parents assured me that I did not need to fully understand illness and death, but I did understand and experience love and help from others.

I believe Pop is in heaven and that I will see him again one day, but hopefully not too soon. In the interim, my attention should be rooted in my limited time on earth in a loving and thankful response to the opportunities of each day along the journey of life and faith.

Chapter 38

Easter for Everyone

So, what is the Easter season all about anyway? It is about being alive instead of dead, making the personal choice to live an authentic, meaningful, loving, and moral life. The choice is always available, and open, along with the potential to enhance and deepen the experience along our journey of life.

I grew up in a conservative Baptist church, which did a lot for me, such as introducing me to the importance and diversity of the Bible and providing some excellent behavioral role models for life. My faith tradition taught me that Easter is a formative event for Christians, which I still wholeheartedly believe. Easter and the belief in the risen and alive-to-us Jesus is the beginning of our Christian faith. As much as I like Christmas, the eyewitness accounts to the resurrection of Jesus as emphasized in the New Testament were the start of my faith tradition. One of the earliest written expressions of this is in 1 Cor 15:1–11, probably written around AD 50–55 (about twenty years after the earthly ministry of Jesus) by Paul to a church he established at Corinth. Paul emphasized (v. 3) that he handed down what he had received, including a list of people who claimed to have had experiences of some kind with Jesus after his death (and Paul was one of them per v. 8). Paul appears to be quoting and citing a very early confessional liturgy or formula familiar to his readers and him. Paul's experience is also recorded in Acts 9, where Jesus "met" him on the road to Damascus, changing Paul's life and in many ways shaping some aspects of Christianity.

In retrospect, what I do not like about my early exposure to Easter is its exclusivity. Yes, personally, I do believe the Easter story. It is foundational to my own faith. Yet I do not see it as a sword to be used for judgment, litmus tests, and exclusivity. I think Easter has something important to say to everyone—that positive change toward a life of service, love, care, and the pursuit of justice is a volitional choice at any point in everyone's life. Those are the traits Jesus himself lived and taught his followers to live out. For Christians, lives with those characteristics are the expected response action to the Easter accounts. We can die to other inauthentic ways of life and change for the better.

Following Jesus is what I think all Christians are called to do. It is our vocation. As Paul or one of Paul's companions tells us in Col 3:12, "As God's chosen ones, holy and beloved, put on [this can also mean 'clothe yourselves with'] compassion, kindness, humility, [gentleness], and patience." For me, "chosen ones" simply means those who choose to follow as disciples. Paul adds, "Above all, [we should] clothe [ourselves] with love, which binds everything together in perfect harmony" (v. 14).

I think Paul is onto something for Christians and everyone in any faith or non-faith tradition. We are free to choose to live in such a way. It is all about our decisions and chosen actions in life situations. From the depths of Auschwitz, Frankl advised that the last of human freedoms in any situation is the ability to choose our attitude in any given set of circumstances. His were extreme and unfathomable, yet he had this life-altering insight as shared in his autobiographical *From Death Camp to Existentialism* (also known by the alternative title

Man's Search for Meaning (Beacon Press 1959)). Authentic and moral intentions can and should result in favorable behavioral modifications.

Easter is the time and reminder of potential true life change for everyone, including in challenging and rewarding times, as well as every season in between. Having to believe certain things happened in an exact way on the first Easter and resulted in certain theological truths ultimately important for God's acceptance (and a ticket after death through the pearly gates) simply misses the point. Easter is about life and response now. Yes, as a Christian, I take comfort in the afterlife component of the Easter message, but it is not a vehicle for judgment. That would contradict what Jesus taught us in the important Sermon on the Mount, the longest of his assembled teachings in the New Testament: "Do not judge, so that you may not be judged" (Mt 7:1). In that same chapter and collection, Jesus puts the emphasis not on calling him "Lord" (v. 21) but on following his teachings and example (vv. 24–27).

Easter is for everyone, multifaceted for Christians and meaningful for all, an opportunity to follow a prime example of love, service, and justice with action.

Chapter 39

Handle Words with Great Care

"With it we bless the Lord and Father, and with it we curse those who are made in the likeness of God. . . . [T]his ought not to be so" (Jas 3:9–10). What is the author of the Book of James, a real treasure in Christian Scripture, talking about? The tongue—our spoken words to each other. In our present day, there are so many diverse ways to "talk." Many of them are quick and wide open for speaking before we think much about what we are saying and its potential consequences, especially of a cursing or denigrating character.

Have you ever said something hurtful to someone and wished for a mulligan (a familiar term for casual golfers with the hope of replacing a bad shot with a good one)? I mean a true do-over, as if the regretful words were never spoken or written. Saying we are sorry and forgiveness (by the recipient and ourselves for what we said) are important bridge builders of relationships, yet the original malicious words linger. With written words, including lightning quick and modern no-thought-necessary communication, there is a stronger record of the language. Quick and thoughtless thumbs can curse as quick, maybe quicker, than the mouth.

With a bad golf shot before an improved mulligan, one can put the first ball into a pocket to hide and forget it, leaving no trace of the errant mistake. This is not true of damaging words that cut into the heart of another and often into our own for what we said.

I still vividly remember something I said to my sweet mother when I was in the first grade. Like many normal kids, I sometimes explored creative ways to stay home from school. I had been mildly sick one day and stayed home, then determined the next morning to try and get two days out of it. My mom easily saw through my pleas and knew I was just fine. Every day the school did not have fish sticks on the menu (which was most days), my mother meticulously and with loving care made the very best sack lunches for me. She knew recess and lunch were the highlights of a school day for me back then and wanted to contribute to these parts of my school day. This was of course more than a decade before I fell in love with school and decided to devote the bulk of my work life to teaching.

On that day, my mother gently made it clear I was going to school and handed me yet another great looking sack lunch. I scowled and said nothing during the short ride in the car with her to school. I should have just stayed quiet. Instead, when we arrived at school, I opened the car door in silence before crushing the sack lunch into the door, saying, "I don't want this!" I pitched it back into the car seat and slammed the door shut. Ten minutes later, my teacher noticed me upset and crying in the classroom. She took me aside and listened to me with care. She understood why I was so upset at being hateful (in my mind) toward my mother. My teacher then called my mother to come get me. She arrived immediately, and I tearfully told her how very sorry I was for what I had done and said. I spent the rest of my day very close to her at home. My mother quickly forgave me. I doubt she spent much more time ever thinking about it, but I never forgot my harsh words.

That is my earliest memory of using hurtful words (and actions) toward others, especially one who I loved so very much. I wish it was the only time in my life I spoke or acted in a harmful way toward another. I have said and done a lot of worse things as an adult. I try each time to apologize and make it right, but there is a sting that lasts, including when we are on the receiving end of hateful words.

In the 1980s tune "Handle with Care" by the Traveling Wilburys, former Beatle George Harrison sings about cleaning up messes he has made. I wish cleaning up and healing from thoughtless and hurtful words could actually be accomplished. Apologies, forgiveness, and changing to loving words and actions go a long way toward it. Better yet, handling all of our words with great care and truly thinking before we speak about what to say, if anything, and its potential impact is a preferable route. In many cases, it is best simply to stay quiet. As the author of the Book of James so wisely says, "[L]et everyone be quick to listen, slow to speak, [and] slow to anger" (1:19).

Chapter 40

The Role of Experience in Our Journeys

Recently, a longtime friend died unexpectedly in a bicycle accident. He and his wife were consistently gentle, caring, and loving people. Do we need to understand from a faith rooted perspective why he died prematurely and arbitrarily?

In Judeo-Christian Scripture, Prv 3:1–2; 8:18 tell us, respectively, that keeping commandments adds "length of days and years of life" and that "[r]iches and honor...[and] enduring wealth" are with those who follow wisdom and good morals. In contrast, the Teacher who is the source of the Book of Ecclesiastes emphatically says, "[T]here are righteous people who are treated according to the conduct of the wicked, and there are wicked people who are treated according to the conduct of the righteous" (Eccl 8:14).

Between these perspectives is the Book of Job. According to the prose prologue and epilogue (Jb 1–2; 42:7–17), an archaic characterization of God and his heavenly court includes a predecessor sort of Satan, the "accuser," who prompts God to test the righteous Job ("blameless and upright . . . and turned away from evil" [1:1]) with suffering, including killing his children (vv. 6–12, 18–19). Per the epilogue, in the end Job gets back family and riches (as if children are fungible and replaceable like grain in a silo [42:10–17]). Sandwiched in the middle is the real emphasis of Job, the poetic portions (3–42:6). Generally, Job questions God about all the bad things happening to him because he is a righteous person. In this heart of the book, Job's so-called friends grill him to inquire about his actual morality, as if he must be guilty of wrongdoing to experience such extreme misfortune.

Although there is more diversity to these three books, with each of them worthy of study and reflection, the basic contrasts are striking. All three are what theologians call Wisdom Literature, which is quite different from other Scripture, such as the books of the Law and the Prophets, in the Hebrew Bible and Christian Old Testament. Generally, wisdom books (especially Proverbs and Ecclesiastes) record and reflect, in part, teachings of a universal nature rooted in life experience, observation of the lives of others, and reflections on such by respected teachers.

How do we make sense of the contrasts? In my view, we don't. Rather, we recognize the differences in perceptions of God. Historically, people of faith understood wealth, a large family, and good health as consequences of ethical behavior, with punishment the result for immoral actions. Many have seriously questioned or outright rejected this traditional theological outlook. Nevertheless, some seem to hold onto it and teach the same even today.

One implicit issue is the role of life experiences, our own and others, in our faith journeys. Scripture, worship, prayer, meditation, teachings, and role models are examples of other faith-related elements. Paying attention to what happens in life, however, is a strong faith-related element and filter of sorts for religious teachings.

When something bad happens in our own or the life of another, such as a painful terminal illness or the loss of a child, where is God? In such circumstances, sometimes "friends" or others claim God has some "plan," insist it will all work out for good, or dismiss it as beyond our understanding. Perhaps they are clinging to a predictable view of God in this life to rely upon. In contrast, life experiences show us that the best of people, like everyone else, are subject to serious health, accident, and other misfortunes.

In Kushner's recent book, *Nine Essential Things I've Learned about Life* (Alfred A. Knopf 2015), Kushner expounds on the belief that "an all-wise, all-powerful God who is totally good must [have] His reasons for inflicting incurable illness on innocent children, reasons beyond . . . comprehension" as "religion done badly." Indeed it is. I like the title of Kushner's book, using nine instead of ten (which seems more complete) things he has learned, because at age eighty-four, he is still observing, seeking, and learning, as we all should be doing.

Returning to the recent death of our friend and his widow, some might say, "It was just his time," as if it was preordained. I disagree and think instead that it triggers our time to comfort and help his wife in her grief, being present actively to care for her.

Where God fits into extreme suffering and grief is not in the causation. Rather, it is embodied in the caring and loving response actions of others in actively helping the sick, grieving, and unfortunate people around us. From a faith perspective, instead of trying to explain and defend the erroneous proposition that God causes bad things to happen to people, we should alter our attention and invest our energy and time in helping those who are suffering, while seeking God's enablement to do so.

Appendix 1

Small Group Experience

For where two or three are gathered in my name,
I am there among them. Mt 18:20

Insight and enablement for a meaningful life are fueled by caring input from special friends as well as consistent, prayerful, and meditative solitude. Small groups with common interests can be excellent mechanisms for sharing ideas and contemplative reflection. In faith-oriented contexts, such groups often are part of or connected in some way to a larger entity. The following is a glimpse into portions of my current and prior experiences with small groups in larger organizations that are and have been an important part of my life.

Like so many small faith-related groups whose members have interacted for years, the Journey class at Highland Park Baptist Church in Austin, Texas, is a special "place." Although we often refer to it as a class, discussion group is more descriptive. It is a fundamental part of my life because of the spiritual benefits of periodic sharing over time with good friends. Additionally, in association with Highland Park, I led an interfaith discussion group called Practical Faith in local coffee shops for three years.

Like any small group in a church (traditionally called a Sunday school class), the Journey class is both one part of a whole as well as a thriving, vital entity itself. Putting the group in context, Highland Park Baptist Church was born as a missionary project of the First Baptist Church of Austin in the 1950s. Currently, Highland Park is a relatively small (typically fewer than one hundred in worship) church with a moderate and inclusive orientation. Like many moderate churches, Highland Park has gone through various identity crises, struggling to define itself and its basic mission.

I am not a fan of a protracted Christian (or any other) self-conscious focus, or worse yet, focus-induced identity crisis. I believe an unusual amount of attention to who we are, for congregations, small groups, or individuals, is an unhealthy detriment and a sign of pride. Our actions define us. Hyper-attention to branding can be more of a root concern that others perceive us in a certain light. From personal experience, when I become overly concerned with the perception of others, it is often with an intention that they not misunderstand me and think I am like someone else whose perspective I really do not like. For example, if I think of myself as a "modern" or "progressive" Christian, I might cringe if anyone misperceived me as a "fundamentalist" or "conservative" Christian (or vice versa). I could get so wrapped up in this that I introduce and describe myself in negative terms: "I go to such and such Baptist church, but we are not fundamentalist or exclusive." In other words, I must convince this person that I am not one of THEM! What a red flag!

Like the people in Corinth that Paul rebuked in 1 Cor 3, I have become more concerned with human categories or factions than with serving God. Jesus taught us to act—to respond to his teachings and follow him—to the point of not letting the "left hand know what [the] right hand is doing" (Mt 6:3). As Paul summarizes, God "created [us] in Christ Jesus for good works" (Eph 2:10). Being a Christian—or in any other faith context, individually and collectively as religious congregations—eclipses our self-conscious sense of identity and how we think others perceive us. This is best reflected in what we do every day, especially how we treat people we encounter in our particular circumstances.

In addition to grappling with our identity and mission at Highland Park, we have struggled with tough issues over the years. Some of these are common to many congregations, including sexual orientation, abortion, and whether flags and similar symbols have any place in a church or other worship setting. At high points, we talked and disagreed with a mutuality of respect. At other times, we clashed, feelings were bruised, and some even left our church. Importantly, however, thinking through issues together generally made us stronger.

Personally, from a faith perspective, I understand how well-intentioned Christians from differing backgrounds and generations can disagree on certain contemporary issues. I cannot begin to comprehend, however, why so many people have a myopic and judgmental litmus test approach toward others, as if any one issue is the only one that really matters, and worse yet, defines who is truly in touch with God. We as Christians spend way too much time and energy on both sides of potentially divisive issues. How refreshing would it be for Christians (along with others) instead to back off, reach out, and pour our collective efforts into actively helping others that we *all* agree are in need?

Fortunately, and more positively regarding Highland Park, in addition to being a thinking church that struggles with important issues, ours is an actively caring church. For example, for decades we have implemented a rock-solid outreach ministry, which we call our Touch Ministry. The heart of our Touch Ministry historically included a person-on-call program wherein church members actively reached out and ministered to those in our congregation and other friends who were ill or otherwise in need. Today, all at Highland Park participate in this ministry. Persons on our "touch list" each week are showered with prayers, and unless they request otherwise, notes, phone calls, and personal visits of encouragement.

In this collective context, we as the Journey class gather each Sunday morning as a diverse group of men and women, ranging over the years together in age from early thirties to ninety-nine. Some of us are married, others single, and some divorced. The ones who are married do not necessarily attend as couples, although we do have some married couples in our class. Some of us have been together for about twenty years, while others are new to our group. There is a wide variation in what we do. Our class has included students, attorneys, medical doctors, engineers, public school teachers, and retirees, among others. Thus, our class is not traditionally structured according to age, gender, or marital status. These common historic bases for small groups can feel forced as well as rooted in more of a social understanding (or misunderstanding) of the reason for gathering regularly to talk about questions and issues related God, religion, and life. In the Journey class, we are joined together in a common quest for a richer, more qualitative Christian life-journey through Bible and other faith-oriented study with open and respectful dialogue.

For me, the Journey class is a high point in a string of positive small group experiences dating back to childhood. My earliest memory of traditional and meaningful Sunday school is as a second grader with my father as my teacher. I learned a reverence for the Bible and the importance of reading it and trying to make reasoned sense of it myself on a consistent basis. I also learned at that early age to talk about what I read, especially to ask questions, and to listen to the questions and opinions of others. My father was always open to questions and discussion. He was also comfortable that some questions themselves were more important than answers. As my first small group leader, he fostered an open and friendly atmosphere that encouraged but did not coerce input. I was never afraid to ask anything or say something that was "wrong" or irreverent. I also sensed the freedom to simply be quiet and listen. Dad would always calmly answer any questions, indicate that he did not know, or suggest the question might not have a definitive answer. Thus, I learned at an early age by example that we can openly and honestly express concerns and questions as well to God as our loving parent. I also learned that one key sign of intelligence and maturity is an ability to say, "I do not know," realizing the contrasting attitude of appearing to know it all or having special knowledge was an indication of potential falsehood.

Beyond childhood, I recall loose affiliations with other faith-oriented classes through high school. After the experience with my dad, my next truly significant experience in a small faith related group was as a college student at the University of Texas in Austin. I attended a college class at a local church for about a year as I began to incorporate academic perspectives into my study of the Bible and religion at UT. My Sunday school teacher, another in a series of teacher friends and models, was a serious student of the Bible who invited our inquiries and input. As a graduate student in religion at Baylor University, I attended and helped lead a similar college class at a downtown church in Waco. In retrospect, these were formative experiences that would feed into the Journey class.

During most of my time in Waco as a graduate student at Baylor, and as an insurance adjuster before deciding to attend law school, our family attended Lake Shore Baptist Church. Our time there was profound. I started to uncover what it truly meant to be a Baptist in the current moderate circle of open and inclusive Baptist churches and what I consider the truly historic Baptist tradition. As opposed to being some alleged "modern" or "liberal" trend away from more conservative churches, I discovered that this "kind" of Baptist was more traditional in exemplifying what we call the "priesthood of the believers," which we hopefully endeavor to live out in the Journey class. Others can define and have described this Baptist rooted concept better than I ever could, but in a nutshell, it means to me that people make their Christian belief and journey *their very own.* As a matter of integrity and authenticity, belief and faith should exist, often with numerous unanswered questions, not because someone else says so, but because of personal *choice*, understanding, and living.

At Lake Shore, I led a Sunday morning group that had a major impact on me. We were a group of people serious about studying the Bible and openly talking about and analyzing it, our day-to-day experiences in life, and our differences of opinion. This group was a true precursor of the Journey class.

Our family moved to Austin in 1989 after I graduated from Baylor Law School. Although we visited Episcopal and Presbyterian churches in exasperation of Baptist politics and fixation on miniscule issues about right and wrong opinions, we soon decided to join Highland Park. I better understand now that there was no immunity from such bickering in any denomination or congregation. We had two compelling reasons to join Highland Park. First and foremost, our children liked it. Additionally, it was similar to Lake Shore in Waco (which we missed). I helped team teach a small college class for a short time before we started the Journey class in 1991. Our makeup and numbers have varied over the years, culminating in our current circle of about fifteen to twenty friends.

Appendix 2

Small Group Values

[A]ll things should be done decently and in order.
1 Cor 14:40

Over the years, particularly in the Journey class, experience taught the importance of guiding principles or values for a constructive and rewarding experience in a small discussion gathering. In the Journey class, we do not post or otherwise articulate any principles. After all, we do not want our freedom and openness to be stifled by a stiff approach to rules. Rather, we generally follow certain guidelines and mutually benefit. The following are suggestions for initial ideas, perhaps operating principles, toward a mature small group experience.

1. **Have a leader.** A group founded on open discussion is great, but without a guide or moderator, it can be chaotic. Thus, every group and each gathering need a leader. There should be one main leader and one or more alternates to assume the role in the leader's absence. A leader can also be thought of as a teacher, but not necessarily so. Oftentimes, the leader is the one who simply starts the engine and occasionally steers the participants back onto the targeted road for discussion and inquiry. As interest directs, rabbit trails should be open for exploration.

2. **Consistently read the Bible (or other significant authoritative point of reference in non-Christian faith settings).** Regardless of the topic of discussion, strive to include a passage of scripture. A biblical passage (or part of another faith tradition's sacred writings or teachings) will often be the focal point of the session and related discussion. At other times, a group might consider a contemporary subject or book. Part of the leader's role is to incorporate appropriate reading, including from the Bible in a church group. It is a good habit, on Sunday and every other morning. If a class is talkative, try reading scripture on the front end before participants get wound up because the class time might expire before the "good book" is opened.

3. **Share concerns and intentionally pray together.** Starting a session with shared concerns and celebrations is an excellent mechanism to gain attention, encourage focus, and build community. This sharing over time should blossom into outreach outside of actual meetings in case of special needs of members or others in the larger group.

4. **Be prepared**. This relates to everyone. The leader should suggest readings and other preparatory material before each time together to give everyone the opportunity to prepare. Preparation should not be burdensome, and there should be no expected outward sign of accountability for it. Nevertheless, encouraging prayerful reading and reflection during the week before coming together is helpful toward forming a good daily habit. Typically, preparation can include one or more biblical passages or book segments that can be read and considered deliberately in ten to fifteen minutes or stretched

into more lengthy preparation as each member desires. The idea is not to create a burden and/or the stress of having to demonstrate preparedness for the next session. Rather, the objective is to afford an opportunity for some degree of intentional preparatory focus. Thus, avoid tests, handouts to complete, or any other forced participation. Instead, encourage consistent and serious Bible and other faith related study with contemplation and attention to actual life experiences, and avoid any risk of embarrassing or alienating participants by calling on them in front of others.

5. **Always be flexible.** Regardless of any plan for a course of study or a particular group session, always be open to the needs of the group and current subjects of importance in your congregation or larger entity, if applicable. For example, years ago our church went through an intentional interim period to consider problems in our recent past, start to heal, and prepare for a new pastor. The experience was grand, due in large part to the excellent leadership of our interim pastor at the time, Ron Higdon from Kentucky. During this phase of our church life, we took frequent opportunity to expand discussions of interim related subjects in our small group, such as talking for a few weeks about our individual ideas related to a church survey for prioritization of characteristics we hoped for in our next pastor.

6. **Allow for open discussion.** Everyone should be encouraged but not made to participate. Open-ended questions by the leader are excellent avenues to encourage discussion. Thus, asking, “What do you think about it?” is preferable to an attitude of, “You agree with my point about this, now don’t you?”

Oral participation should be voluntary. Avoid calling on anyone who has not indicated a desire to speak. Part of a truly open dialogue is affording individuals the opportunity to simply be quiet and appreciate everyone else's input. *Never* force anyone to share personal thoughts or feelings. Rather, cultivate an atmosphere where everyone can relax and truly sense the freedom to speak up or keep silent.

7. **Be prepared to listen more than you talk.** This is tough for a lot of folks. A small group is an excellent setting for learning and exercising such a skill. When you speak, be calm, respectful, and attentive to others who want to join in. Avoid showing up with an agenda. Do not monopolize any discussion. Stay off of any soapbox. After all, one's goal should not be to convince others that a particular position on an issue is "correct" and others must agree.

   We learn, and God speaks to us, in so many ways, including from consideration of prayerful insights from others. When others speak, do not just hear the sounds or plan ahead your own response. Rather, truly listen and avoid interruption. At the end of each session, how class participants treated one another will be more important than each member having every question and issue presented allegedly resolved. Resolving all issues would not be much fun anyway. What would you do next week? We should keep exploring our faith and related issues. More importantly, in response to such exploration and study, we should actively love and respect our sisters, brothers, and others.

8. **Respectfully disagree and allow others to do the same.** Open discussion means variation of opinion. Welcome this. Phrase your opinions, even the strongest held ones, as your beliefs or thoughts as opposed to "the way it is." Gently and peacefully allow others to have different views.

Some people of faith are afraid of new or different ideas, especially for someone *else* to hold. Our faith and related beliefs are chosen, not coerced. We elect to believe and act in the first instance. We choose to be Christian or follow another faith tradition or similar path because that is who we want to be and what we want to do. Any "proof" of the reality of our faith most certainly flows from active expressions in life, such as caring for and loving others and experiencing the peace and wholeness God can give us.

About the Author

Walt Shelton is one of the most read faith columnists in Texas over the past decade, writing countless columns for the *Austin American-Statesman*. He has also given numerous presentations and written legal articles over the years, with some of them stemming from column readers' invitations to speak on subjects captivating their attention. For example, a long-standing and inclusive organization called CWU, formed in the 1940s to unite black and white Christian women to work toward unified caregiving, asked Walt to address their group after reading one of his columns focused on social/biblical justice. As a result, he addressed a large audience of half white and half black women on World Community Day in 2017 about this important subject and initiative, drawing heavily on the Book of Amos. Other articles led to opportunities to speak to certain church groups. On these and many more occasions, attendees complimented his columns, showed him ones they had cut out and kept in their Bibles and other places, and strongly encouraged him to continue writing.

In legal circles, Walt has focused in recent years speaking and writing primarily on ethical topics related not only to applicable standards for attorneys but also to balancing quality of life considerations and other personal priorities in such a demanding and sometimes overwhelming profession.

A Professor at Baylor Law School, nationally recognized Environmental and Water Law attorney and noted speaker, Walt is passionate about empowering others through knowledge and encouragement. On occasion, he hears from current and former students about his faith and life related columns in the *Statesman*. For example, in a recent course evaluation from a student at Baylor, she added to her general comments section at the end that "we all read your articles in the paper" and "please keep on writing."

Walt graduated first in his class from Baylor Law with a JD in 1989, where he was the Editor-in-Chief of the *Baylor Law Review*. This was quite an accomplishment. He was thirty years old, married, and with two young children and a mortgage when he left a successful job to start law school. Although he was a full-time student (the only option at Baylor), he also worked part time, coached his son's soccer team, spent all of the time he could with his family, and led a small discussion-oriented Sunday school class in order to balance and maintain his priorities.

Walt holds a BA in History from the University of Texas (1977, summa cum laude), where he was admitted to Phi Beta Kappa and Phi Eta Sigma, and an MA in Religion from Baylor University (1979, magna cum laude). His undergraduate degree substantively was a disguised religion degree. He combined religious history, Jewish studies and philosophy, the Bible as history, critical and analytical biblical and other courses keyed into religion (such as Biblical Archeology and the History of Religion in America), ancient Greek, and Hebrew in his elective-friendly BA. His objective in creating this network of excellent courses was a strong foundation from a public, nationally known, and excellent university for graduate work in religion.

Walt focused primarily on biblical studies in his MA in religion, his first Baylor degree, hoping then to pursue a PhD in religion and teach at the university level. He started his PhD with a full-ride scholarship, but personal plans with his wife to start a family while still very young in their mid-twenties became more important to them. This necessitated full-time financial support, and he happily put time with his expanding family as his top priority. However, Walt never lost his keen sense of vocation as a teacher, educator, and lifetime student of the Bible and religious matters. At the time, he never imagined law school would be a vehicle toward achieving his goals. Walt's highest passion for religious education and leadership materialized further after law school, when he focused his attention on writing and speaking in addition to his continued leadership of small discussion groups.

Walt has taught at Baylor Law School since 1990. He currently teaches four environmental and water-related courses. He also supervises externships at federal and state agencies, directs independent studies, and sponsors the Baylor Environmental and Natural Resource Law Society. Perhaps more significantly, Walt has an open-door policy and readily meets with and counsels students. Additionally, he maintains contact with many of his former students, as both a friend and mentor. Walt also taught Business Law in the Baylor Hankamer School of Business (1999–2001) and the McCombs School of Business at the University of Texas in Austin (2006).

Walt devotes substantial time in service to the legal profession in Texas. He is cochair and former chair of the law school committee of the Environmental and Natural Resources Law Section (ENRLS) of the State Bar of Texas. He is also a member of the executive committee of ENRLS, serving as part of this group for more than a decade. In his work on the law school committee, for years Walt has created, moderated, and participated in law school Environmental and Water Law programs for all accredited law schools in Texas. Thus, he has met and influenced countless law students across the state for many years.

As an attorney, Walt practiced in the past as part of prominent environmental practice groups with Baker Botts, L.L.P. and Haynes and Boone, L.L.P. Although he still maintains a small law practice on his own in Austin, focusing on transactional and regulatory matters, Walt now spends almost all his law-related work life teaching, working with students, writing, speaking, and contributing to education in a service role through ENRLS activities. He is known by many in the legal community for expertise in the remediation of contaminated properties, Brownfield programs (i.e., cleaning up and redeveloping previously used properties to maximize green space), and water quality. His peers have consistently recognized him for excellence in practice, including being named in The Best Lawyers in America for the past twenty consecutive years (currently in the areas of Environmental Law and Water Law).

Walt is married to Roxanne Shelton, and they have two children, five grandchildren, and one very special dachshund, all in the Austin area.

To learn more, visit www.WaltShelton.com.